MURDER IN

MURDER IN MIND

Investigations from a
Yorkshire crime writer's casebook

Stephen Wade

Scratching Shed Publishing Ltd

For Cathy

Contents

PREFACE

•

About the Book

MURDER IN MIND was written at a point in my life at which I reached several milestones in terms of developing as a storyteller. Before that I dabbled and messed about with words. But now I have become a crime writer in both fact and fiction and have attempted something of a distillation of approaches and ideas here. It also adds more of a dimension of reflection, as I have fused case narratives with new enquiries. I began as a poet and writer of short fiction 20 years ago and, after academic study discovered the fascination of telling stories from real, recorded human experience. I recall that on the day after my last English finals exam, I sat in the garden reading the stories of Chekhov and marking passages with a red pen. That couldn't be what reading was all about – nor writing. As Sherwood Anderson memorably advised: 'Stop playing around with words and write something.'

Going into teaching, I was asked to contribute

something to a book on Bradford. I researched the life of a local writer, James Burnley and, in the course of it, found a long account of his visit to Wakefield prison around 1880. It was a revelation to me. There was something about the mix of a documentary voice and the closeness to the earthy, repressed souls behind those bars that enchanted me and fired me to write about transgression in times gone by, when retribution and 'correction' were the ideological bases of prison. A few years later I edited a book in the same series on Huddersfield, and after that came my first true crime book, *Foul Deeds and Suspicious Deaths in Halifax*. To be frank, I had little idea whilst working on it what research into crime and law was really like – how deeply it could go. It became a learning experience.

I began to see that looking into transgression offered a very special insight, there is nothing like 'sin' for shining a light on the network of values which sustain a community. I was smitten. My reading spread into the social history of crime and works that helped understand the complex areas of study related to forensics, which in derivation means 'relating to a court and a trial', together with complex motives for crime. My good friend, ex-detective Stuart Gibbon, tells me that humiliation is the most common motive for murder. That word resonates with the shiver of potential plots.

This book is a new departure for me, one with three strands: reflections on crime writing of all kinds, case studies from my files re-examined, and autobiographical accounts of meetings with those involved in crime research. I have come to see that the more literary end of the true crime spectrum is where the depth of interest lies, especially the oft-returned to question of why is murder so compelling. What must also be borne in mind is that a terrible crime in 1400 may be no more than a misdemeanour in 1960.

I can offer one notable factor I would call truly original: my look at the murderess from Leeds, Louie Calvert. Here, I beg to differ with the accepted wisdom. I have given the reader a steady, close account into what I consider to be a tale in which a woman was hanged for murder when, in fact, she very probably never planned to kill anyone. The cliché is that every person behind bars insists that they are innocent but in Louie Calvert's case, I genuinely believe this to be true.

The cases I have revisited mostly persist as being mysteries. Many are open to fresh investigation and a select few are fated to remain unsolved such as those of Bill o'Jacks, Mr Blum and Emily Pye. Over the years some cases are at first intriguing and their potential for a fully developed story is evident, others never really offer more than one dynamic scene. Then there are the Louie Calvert tales, as complex as the most intricate and absorbing thriller. I have also included something on the nature of the 'criminous' – a word invented to explain the fascination of crime.

What first opened my eyes to the nature of criminous thinking was the discovery of what was Britain's best specialist bookshop for criminal reading, Clifford Elmer Books. Clifford was from York but settled in Manchester and his catalogues typified the excitement of discovering both titles and crime ephemera such as cigarette cards and pamphlets, but also rare contemporary accounts of 'horrible murder' by anonymous scribblers. It was in Elmer's pages that I saw the storytelling potential of the crimes and misdemeanours of times past.

The following pages will give the reader an account of one investigator's passions and obsessions, as an armchair detective who occasionally stood up and went out there.

WRITING CRIME AND THE FASCINATION OF DEVIANCE

I was sitting in Fred Wade's bookshop in Halifax, signing copies of my book on Calderdale crime. Unusually for me there was a long queue waiting for my attention. But from the corner of my eye I could see a woman loitering by the counter, talking to the assistant and looking across, trying to catch my attention. The people patiently in line seemed to want to talk, after all, it was a Saturday and there was a leisurely feeling in the air, along with some reluctant Yorkshire sunshine.

Three or four times I glanced across at her, she seemed to be agitated and because she looked at me, I felt that there was some link with her emotional state. The last person in the queue took a signed book and sloped off. I looked up, and the nervous customer had gone. The shop assistant came over and said: 'That lady wanted to talk to you... she said it was about Emily Pye' - perhaps the most mythic unsolved murder in Halifax.

On Whitsun Saturday 1957, detective superintendent Herbert Hannam and detective sergeant Rowe, both of the Yard, were on their way north to Halifax. They had been called in by the town's chief constable soon after the body of Emily Pye was discovered, brutally murdered, in the house behind her grocer's shop on Gibbet Street. Emily, aged 80, had been severely bludgeoned to death in what one officer described as, 'A rain of blows to the head' by a ruthless killer.

The town end of Gibbet Street today is in the heart of the Asian community, there is a mosque quite near to the shop which still stands. The streets around are crowded and busy. The thoroughfare of Gibbet Street leads down to the centre of the town and is always noisy. In 1957 it was not as busy but it is easy to imagine what it was like then, as the red-brick terraces still stand and Back Rhodes Street, in which her home stood and where she was killed, is still there, unchanged. To visit the place, with the knowledge of that killing, is to invite a shudder of irony that such an horrendous homicide should happen in so banal a place.

It was a Saturday when she died. Police later found that the shop and the house had been locked from around 1.45pm. Her body was discovered when her niece Doris Wilson and her husband Derek had come from Northowram to invite Emily to spend some of the holiday with them. But they found the premises locked and, through a window, Derek saw the old lady's body, covered with a rug.

The whole investigation was dramatic and high-profile. The forensic specialists came, including professor Tryhorn from the Science Laboratory in Harrogate. Crowds gathered to watch as officers began their enquiries. It was a senseless murder, apparently done for a small amount of money taken from the till. It became clear that another, more substantial stash of cash was hidden on the premises and had not been discovered. Superintendent Hannam said he would not have been able to find it. The murder seemed to have been opportunist, not by anyone who knew her and the initial line centred on a chance passing customer, perhaps en route to Lancashire.

It was unusual for such a high-ranking officer to be there. Hannam was very highly thought of; a smart, dapper man, wearing a Homburg and a very expensive suit. A picture in the local *Halifax Courier* shows him almost posing for the camera, looking dignified and impressive. Then 47, he had been a leading figure in many West End cases and had been on assignments abroad, notably investigating monetary fraud in the USA. Such detail was given about Herbert Hannam that readers of the local papers were told that he wore 'designer' clothes and that his son was highly educated. A photograph of him taken in 1957 shows a solidly-built man, quite short, with a military bearing. He wears a trilby and a three-piece suit and his shoes shine with a regimental sparkle. It is an image of a man who means business. Hannam was interviewed almost as if he were a *Boy's Own* hero and was, undoubtedly, a remarkably interesting figure to find walking the streets of a northern industrial town.

The affair reached almost mythic status in the area for some time, the very name Emily Pye becoming synonymous with an unsolved murder.

She had been such a popular and warm-hearted woman, running the shop more as a hobby than anything else having been there for 45 years, the last 15 alone after her life-long companion had died. All the more horrible, then, that such a kind and sociable woman should perish in such a manner. The plain, low-key figure of Emily Pye attracted in her death a media frenzy and a host of law officers who became local celebrities overnight.

Considerable force was used to kill her and was representative of a template killing across the country. In the early to mid-1950s there had been a stream of such attacks on lonely women living alone, often on commercial premises. But nothing came of the enquiry and it remained unsolved until a death-bed confession given to Calderdale Police in 2004, although the full details of that have not been released. Superintendent John Parker told the *Halifax Courier*: 'This man made a number of anonymous calls. He told the newspaper that his father had admitted to Emily's murder two or three days before he had died. The caller refused to give details because his mother was still alive at the time and unaware of her husband's secret.' The man added that his father had said what he had done was not worth the anguish he had gone through. In 2006 police again appealed for the caller to come forward with full details, but as yet there is no closure.

So, what about the woman in the queue? The bookshop assistant added: 'She thinks she knows who killed her!' But she was long gone and her story with her. The upshot of the saga, though, is that I had another story to tell, that of Inspector Hannam, whose character is endlessly fascinating. It turns out that 'The Count' – as he was known – was involved in several prominent cases including the 'Bicycle Murder of Barbara Songhurst' at Teddington Lock, and another murder confession from inside the walls of Walton prison, Liverpool. He really hit the headlines when he was involved in an alleged police corruption investigation.

The Emily Pye story exemplifies one of the frustrations of writing and researching true crime, I lost a real coup but gained a subject of real interest. My interest in such people and cases was initially piqued by two of my uncles from Leeds who both died dramatic deaths.

The first, Jack Schofield, was the kind of charismatic avuncular relative everyone should have. He was small, wiry, a chain-smoking, whiskey drinker living on jokes and tall tales. When he came to visit, the kids gathered. They expected to be teased and told white lies, he was a wonderful raconteur. In his later years, he lived in Armley, still unmarried. He had at one time been engaged but that never worked out. His end was in the fall of a cigarette and a burning building.

The second uncle, Fred, was from Churwell. My recollection of the months or so before he died was that he turned up at our house in Roundhay one day, clothed in a massive orange overcoat that stank of mothballs. He was tall, thin and ginger-haired. Of all the brothers in my father's large family, he was the odd one physically, dashing yet somehow mysterious. You remembered very few of his words and rather more than normal of his looks and movements. That day in 1958 when he visited, though I never knew, he was asking for money.

Fred was in the grip of a criminal act. He had embezzled funds from a working men's club. His destiny was to place his head in an oven and exit, desperately. His sad tale turned out to be something notorious and although the details were kept from the press there remained a stigma. These two deaths, both 'suspicious' grabbed my attention when I became a crime researcher. I was working on a book tracing criminal ancestors and I began to wonder if I had any such skeletons in my cupboard. Until 1961, not only was suicide an offence, it was a felony. That meant that the offender's goods and possessions were forfeited to the state. Yes, you could take your own life, the thinking went, but your life is God's and if you are rash enough to subsume the Almighty's place then be prepared for losses and privations. Felony, as something different from a misdemeanour, was abolished by the Criminal Law Act of 1967.

There was another Leeds murder that attracted family attention. It was the case of David Dewar in 1945. He had been killed in his drive at home, on Beeston Road. Dewar was a doctor and he liked the ladies. He had been having an affair with a married woman, Laura Walker, while her husband was away. Thomas Richardson, a friend of Laura's, decided that some kind of justice should be meted out and at the end of April that year, he killed Dewar. My mother remembered the case well as she was living in Beeston then and she knew a man who had walked past the end of the drive and seen Dewar's body. A brutal murder so close to home was bound to send fear through the streets and the name of Dewar lodged in the memory. It also used to amaze me, in my teens, that stories from so long ago could still be in conversation. The commonest example was that of Dr Crippen, whose name became in itself a dark and sordid byword for the killer in the cellar.

Much of my Leeds childhood and teenage years had such a backdrop. George Orwell in his essay, *The Decline of the English Murder,* discusses the fascination of the everyday reader with both homicide and hanging and how they so often brought out excitement in an otherwise hum-drum existence. The thrill from the classic hangman's tale is never more powerful than when an innocent is either sent to the rope or escapes their fate in the nick of time.

Legislation enacted in 1907, with the founding of the appeals court, made such incidences and story lines more accessible to the masses, adding a fascinating dimension to crime writing. Previously, appeals were only allowed on a point of law which was then put before a group of judges at the Crown Cases Reserved court or to the superior courts by way of magistrates or other officials. But the Act was truly revolutionary, giving any person indicted an unrestricted right of appeal and it included all cases, whether tried at assizes or in quarter sessions. That meant that there could be a challenge on legal procedure, submission of new evidence, on the sentence itself or the verdict.

There were to be three High Court judges sitting on appeal and it is not difficult to imagine the sense of drama and expectancy in such a court. The great lawyers and advocates were much in demand in this context. It needs to be remembered that the personality as well as the skills of the advocate were essential in the nineteenth century, when the accused in any kind of trial could not speak. Lord Birkett wrote of one of the very best of these men, Edward Marshall Hall. 'I listened to his every word with a fascinated wonder and amazement. When he came to his peroration and depicted the figure of justice holding the scales until the presumption of innocence was put there to turn the scale in favour of the prisoner, not only was the jury manifestly impressed, but they indeed… were under a kind of spell.'

· But there was no jury in the court of appeal and the High Court judges were hard nuts to crack. In the early years of the court, many of the homicide cases before them were murders of wives by husbands or lovers by the supposedly beloved. Consequently, the records of the court make compulsive reading as every facet of human relationships is there under scrutiny. There was opposition to this new legal process but just before the law was passed there had been the case of Adolf Beck, a Norwegian in London who had been convicted and given a long prison sentence but who turned out to be a case of mistaken identity. Most realised that a less restricted right of appeal was essential after such suffering by an innocent man.

With this in mind, when I started crime writing in earnest, I could see how much potential there was in a story in which the plaintiff stood in court, often witnessing a last attempt to save his skin by his lawyers and the result of that hearing would determine whether he lived or died. The Court of Criminal Appeal reports were, I discovered, a short story anthology in multiple volumes. Strangely, the protagonist stood, as it were, off-stage, listening to the verbal jousting of the legal representatives and almost helpless. When investigating murder cases, I often reached for the Appeal Court record first and could then work backwards, better reconstructing events and motives.

I was always keen to find notable lawbreakers who hailed from Leeds or Yorkshire in general. Dick Turpin, Peter Sutcliffe and Harold Shipman are amongst the most 'well known,' their deeds recorded worldwide, but there are others who have written a page in the crime casebooks. Owney Madden, made famous as a principal character in Hubert Selby's *The Gangs of New York*, is one such.

Born in Somerset Street in Leeds in 1891, his father went to the States and died there, leaving Owney behind in a children's home at Springfield Terrace off Shadwell Lane until his passage could be arranged in 1902. He rose to become a major player in the prohibition years, running the Cotton Club at one time. Bootlegging and boxing kept him busy for most of his criminal career. I often wonder if he thought of Leeds and what he learned there to enable him to become a gangland villain.

Also overseas were the Thompson brothers, Ben and Billy from Knottingley; Ben being the elder, born in 1842 and Billy three years later. The family emigrated to Austin, Texas and after military service in the Civil War, Ben began a life of adventure. He was involved in 14 considerably violent gunfights but also working, as many fighters did, as a law officer at times. As well as being handy with a gun, he was also a dandy, a colourful character across several states. He was shot dead eventually in a scrap on 11th March, 1884 in San Antonio, Texas.

Billy had a similar journey, begun when he killed a soldier in 1868. He rubbed shoulders with several famous gunslingers including Bat Masterson and Wild Bill Hickok, and one of Billy's lady-friends, Molly Brennan, was killed during a gunfight when Bat faced up to Sergeant King. In June, 1880, Billy was seemingly mortally wounded as he took five bullets but he recovered and escaped. Eight years later fate caught up with him and he died in Laredo.

When it comes to Leeds itself, early in my writing when I was working in the archives, I discovered, one of the city's most significant murder cases recorded pre-1900; the story of William Dove. After reading about him, I couldn't resist walking around the city centre, looking for traces of his presence and that of the shadowy mountebank who egged him on to murder.

In one of the most sensational cases and trials in nineteenth century Leeds, William Dove, a young man from a Methodist family, was led to kill his wife. At the centre of the scandal was Dove's relationship with Leeds 'wizard' Henry Harrison, a man whose medical practice did far more harm than good. As Owen Davies noted when he examined the case: '…nearly all the relevant court records are lost. The assize depositions are missing from the boxes… and there are no surviving Leeds coroners' papers for the period.' Yet Davies reconstructed the incredible story.

Dove was a descendent of farming stock from around

Newby Wiske in North Yorkshire. When his family moved to Leeds, a cholera epidemic was prevalent but the city was expanding thanks to new industries of wool and engineering, tanning and cloth manufacture. It was a good time for entrepreneurs, however, unfortunately that meant dishonest men also had opportunity. Henry Harrison was one such and he came across Dove, realising there was a good chance of profiting from someone who was mentally unstable and yet had wealth as well as a rocky marriage.

Dove had failed as a farmer and when settled with his new wife in the city, his marital relations deteriorated, so enter Harrison, with apparent professional skills that would help. He was a so-called 'wise man' – characters who were amazingly popular with ordinary folk at the time, being mixtures of astrologer, physician and personal guru. Advice involved chemicals and the use of poisons, in Dove's case strychnine administered to his betrothed and, tragically, the best efforts of real medical practitioners could not save Harriet Dove.

Harrison was destined to steal the limelight, he had the gift of the gab, and Dove was an easy victim who was eventually tried at York Summer Assizes in July, 1856. We know that he was hanged 'in front of St George's Field' on 9th August that year and the mystery about that occasion is who hanged him? None of the usual hangmen was able to do the job so the High Sheriff had to advertise for a replacement and he got Thomas Askern who had been overseer of the poor at Maltby, although he denied it in the press. Nevertheless, as Davies notes, 'He was as big a liar as he was a debtor.'

With all this in mind as background, I have written and researched the social history of crime and the biographies of criminals and legal professionals for many years. I now know that the basis of work in the genre is in that strange region which lies somewhere between actual criminal investigation by professionals and the universal fascination with human transgression which percolates through literature. We only have to think of how integral criminal deviance is to such classics as *Crime and Punishment, Oliver Twist, Tom Jones, Hamlet, Thérèse Raquin, Jude the Obscure* and many, many more. There are crime novels and novels about crime; but there are also major works, by any standard, which depend for their narrative heart on some kind of transgression. In the great Greek epic, *The Iliad*, the storyline depends on an abduction.

The theme of this book is the exploration of that blurred area somewhere between social history and the nature of those true crime tales and fictional works which have highlighted a place and a time, as well as offering insights into why and how people transgress, in this case in the county of the Broad Acres. At the heart of it is a paradox and it has to do with the reader's sharing of the story mixed with the fantasy of deviance.

This is perfectly illustrated by a line drawing in an anonymous work of 1912, Palmer, *The Rugeley Poisoner*. It shows a dapper, dandyish man, top-hatted, holding a torch. He appears to be a detective, but the strangeness of the image is that he is smiling, and surrounded by acanthus leaves. He could almost be the MC or ring-master of what is between the covers. Thus, at its very heart, a crime investigation story and the foul murder it chronicles, is both entertainment and diversion, and, dare it be said, escapism.

One man who fully understood that was Alfred Hitchcock. In his film, *Shadow of a Doubt* (1943), an innocent young woman is tormented by her belief that her uncle Charlie from back East is in fact the 'Merry Widow Killer,' whilst her father and his friend constantly ruminate on methods of murder and discuss famous crimes from their favourite 'horrible murder' magazines. To them, psychopaths and hangmen are simply part of an unreal parlour game or a hobby, as innocent and harmless as a round of golf. Hitchcock knew about that intangible connection between nasty murderous reality and the mind-games of imagined crime, the magnetic charm of dark fantasy and how it appeals to the mundane world and its frustrated inhabitants.

True crime and crime fiction rely on insights into why people cross the line into criminality. Having known plenty of criminals, although desperation and poverty play a part, the thrill and risk involved are also prominent characteristics. My impression has always been that the old school villains, the ones we think of when we watch The Italian Job and the 'old lags' who more recently undertook the major robbery at Hatton Garden, absolutely love the challenge of a job, and equally they relish the subculture that goes with it. We can see these perceptions clearly in many gangster films but more evidently in the hagiography given to the Krays and their milieu.

To understand the pull of crime, it pays to examine the notion of the bourgeois illusion of rationality. That is, the good guy has to win, the bad one has to be punished and reason must prevail. There has to be order at the closure of the story. A look at the beginnings of crime stories opens up the interesting structure of process in the early days, before legislation of the 1820s reduced the number of capital crimes significantly. The narrative structure most usually incorporated horrible murder, the investigation and capture of the rogue, their trial and, finally, their execution or at the very least transportation, and a very long time behind bars. That train of events had its absolute dynamic moment in the trial and verdict. In the court process, the public would be treated to first-person accounts of the bloody deed and the killer standing there before them in the dock, silent up to the end, often with the judge donning his black cap and giving out the sentence of death.

When these stories began to be fictionalised, or told factually in the narratives of the jail 'ordinaries' – the turnkeys – the drama was already there, built into the reality. At the base of all this is Aristotle's notion of tragedy; that it must communicate 'pity and fear' and that the tragic hero must be 'like us but not of us' – and that the villain should not go unpunished. Detectives were established in 1842 and although they were at first seen as a threat, part of a police state, they became the upholders of order and instruments of retribution. There was nothing worse, in the days of the penny dreadful tales, than a story in which the criminal got away with it. Attitudes also changed in 1877, when a very prominent Old Bailey trial involved a bunch of corrupt sleuths.

Behind every writer there are influences and in my case it is the master investigator of the courts, the doyen of true crime writers, William Roughead. He was a Scottish legal professional and a wonderfully talented writer in matters 'criminous' as he expressed it. For me, the word denotes that unreality, a bizarre fictionality, which invades crime writing. In 1913 Henry James wrote to his friend Roughead, (pronounced rock-heed) after receiving the latter's volume on Scots trials. James wrote: 'Most interesting and attaching is the book which has held my attention charmed, and your manner of presentation is so strong and skilful that one casts about with open appetite for more such outstanding material into which you may be moved to bite – or at least to make us bite.'

Roughead's narratives of crimes and courtroom dramas, begun in 1906, draws the reader into the intrigue and raises irresistibly complex questions about serious crime throughout history.

Roughead became much admired as an editor of case books on several of the most celebrated trials in criminal history. He was fascinated by the specific insights given to us by crime history, expressive ways of understanding the nature of human transgression. He took the cases so seriously and deepened the nature of the crime writer's enquiry into motivation and circumstance. That is what attracted Henry James to his writing and it is what has confirmed and maintained his reputation. When the *New York Review of Books* published *Classic Cases* in 2000, the editor Luc Sante pointed out that there is another element in a Roughead crime case book. 'Virtually all the hallmarks of the classic British mystery appear here, the apparent originals of those overly clever poisonings, those horrors in sleepy priories and dramas set against majestic Highland backdrops...'

His most effective and comfortable form in his extensive body of work was the extended essay, a length of around 80 pages, and the ingredients were generally a mix of reflection, summary of facts and interpretation of the central story. It was Roughead who did much to popularise and promote the classic Scottish horrors of Burke and Hare, the body-snatchers, and Deacon Brodie, the killer with the double life who was the inspiration for Robert Louis Stevenson's *Dr Jekyll and Mr Hyde*. When Roughead edited and assembled such large-scale cases, he had the power and skill to elucidate all the elements of the scene, from the legal professionals to the investigation process.

Roughead was aware of the seminal essay by Thomas de Quincey, *On Murder Considered as one of the Fine Arts* (1827) and he wrote his own explanation of the appeal of true crime and of murder stories in particular. In his essay, *Enjoyment of*

Murder he has much to say on the compelling nature of the murder trial. 'Every foot of ground should be stubbornly contested, the issue of the fight be uncertain, and the fortunes of the combatants vary from day to day,' he noted. He understood the heady fusion of terror and professionalism at the heart of a courtroom drama. In explaining his art, Roughead was modest, claiming all he intended to do was, '... tell a tale of crime well and truly; to provide the psychologically minded with reliable grist for their recondite mills...' Essentially, taking readers into the actions of monsters and the fateful wrong decisions of the sad and feckless who end up in the dock facing retribution.

William Roughead was born in Edinburgh in 1870. When his father drowned at sea off the Scilly Isles in 1887, the family business was sold. William began his studies in law at Edinburgh University, but did not graduate. He had been articled to a law firm in George Street and having a comfortable income from the sale had no need to follow the normal route into a professional career. He'd acquired an interest in criminal trials and that became his primary concern, forming the basis of his future success in writing. Despite the aborted course of his legal studies, Roughead entered the law by another route when he became a writer to the signet. The word 'writer' here was just a very dated term for 'lawyer' and the post was linked to the status of the private seal of Scottish kings. He was, to all intents and purposes, a solicitor, his name appearing in the official Scottish Law List. From his time as a student through to 1949, three years before his death, he was there in the Edinburgh High Court whenever there was a trial for murder.

To the aficionado of crime and courtroom analysis, the *Notable Trials* series is a template of excellence. Published by Harry Hodge, Roughead's friend, they first got together on a volume about Dr Edward Pritchard, a Glasgow doctor who poisoned his wife and mother-in-law. Roughead's role was editor and it set the standard for what was to follow, such was his expertise and depth of knowledge. He also had the necessary research skills. The *Trials* series' value to the lawyer, historian and medical practitioner is beyond dispute, but its greatest attribute lies in its interest for the general public. The first two volumes were on Madeleine Smith and The trial of the Glasgow Bank Directors, both selling at five shillings. By the end, the series covered the years 1586 to 1953. From 1921 the whole list was compiled as *Notable British Trials*.

Roughead dealt with some of the most infamous and thoroughly explored criminal cases, including those on Oscar Slater (1910) and John Merrett (1929).

These volumes have virtual transcripts of the trials and include illustrations and photographs which are difficult to obtain elsewhere. The secret of their success was partly that they were taken seriously and respected by members of the legal profession as well as read by enthusiasts. In a number of the murder cases he wrote about, there was the added sensational element of unsolved cases or the miscarriage of justice. In the story of John Merrett, who was charged with matricide, he tells one of the most notorious cases of police mishap and inadequacy of investigation, with the particularly Scottish verdict of 'not proven' the result. Roughead was in court at the trial of Oscar Slater and his opinion was that the real killer, Dr Charteris (who was also suspected by Conan Doyle) had an accomplice who hid in the building where the victim was, and it has since become clear that Slater's sentence was wrong.

Roughead's various collections tend to be miscellanies but what he provides is a unity in his narrative voice and his use of contrasts. He took a real pride in his compilations and it is clear that he was concerned that major themes such as the contextual elements in the story – domestic, psychological or merely mundane and banal motivations – were adequately covered. It is high commendation that the prestigious literary publishers, Faber and Faber, published two collections of his case books in the late 1930s. These also had other additional material, thus awarding the crime writer a certain importance and gravitas normally given to poets or essayists.

In the many letters written to Roughead by Henry James we find the affection and respect James gave to a man he saw as a writer just as culturally aware and articulate as himself. The letters are peppered with James's insights into Roughead's virtues: perceptiveness in human nature, an ability to explain and examine motivation under duress, and cruelty as seen in extreme violence. In other words, the crime writer had understanding in relation to human society in a way comparable to that of the novelist.

In Roughead's essays for the academic journal, *The Juridical Review*, we see the future literary stylist. The review was for legal professionals but such was its charm and appeal that it had a broad remit and there was a place for a crime writer with a professional angle on such matters as points of law, procedure and technicalities of the judicial process. In the opening of his essay Physic and Forgery in the journal for 1924, for instance, we have: 'When I was a small boy in Edinburgh the Sunday afternoon walk with my people was a weekly institution. We were Scottish Episcopalians – unlovely label – and as such free to enjoy fresh air and exercise even on the Sabbath.' From Roughead I learned that crime writing and the seduction of transgression can attain the heights of literary fiction.

Then there is Yorkshire as my backdrop; from Whitby to Wetwang, Sheffield to Scarborough. Historically, the epicentre has been York and one of the biggest mysteries was in a painting by the Regency satirist, Thomas Rowlandson, whose biography I wrote in 2010. He recreated an horrific scene featuring a young woman having a noose arranged around her neck by a hideous hangman. Beneath this was written, 'Mary Evans, hanged at York, 1797.' I was writing a chronicle, so I needed the story behind it. After much slaving through various archives, I drew a blank. There was no such girl and no such hanging. What was the painting all about then? My theory is that it was Tom Rowlandson expressing his disgust and making a point for all those who packed the yards around the scaffolds of the land, especially the three-legged mare on the Knavesmire to the eerie spot (now a car park, often flooded) at St George's Field.

This then is a memoir of a writing life as well as an account of a preoccupation with deviance.

The bookish habit started late with me as I was a slow reader in my junior school at Halton Moor, just down a slope from the Temple Newsam estate. The formative book in this transformation was one of the most profound crime fictions of them all, Stevenson's *Dr. Jekyll and Mr Hyde*. Here was the quintessential double morality tale transposed into a compelling thriller. It dawned on me that what you saw in a person was not all there was and, indeed, there could well be a monster or at least a wounded soul somewhere deep within. I saw that acts committed in daily life when someone was 'not himself' could be a deeper concept than ever such a cliché suggested.

Experimenting with the sensation of drunkenness in mid-1960s Leeds, I began to understand the nature of that strange loss of faculties, reason and conformity that crime writing has as its stock-in-trade. Then, around 1967, working in Lewis's department store on The Headrow, in the packing section, I had my first opportunity to have an insight into crime. It was very small at first but led to the fringes of gangland. A lively young married Scot showed me 'a good trick.' He lifted his shirt to show a woman's dress beneath. 'A wee pressy for the little woman!' He chuckled. Needless to say, the staff searches on leaving the store at the end of a working day were none too thorough. That led to my innocent interest in the lives of petty criminals that this work colleague and his mates exemplified, and one day after work I was invited out to a Briggate pub – one with a shady reputation at the time. I settled down amongst a gang of work colleagues who were more than ordinarily conversant with the features of various firearms and other weapons. I didn't see it at the time, but it was useful information for a crime writer.

The word unsolved lies at the heart of the motivations of the study sleuth, we need closure, a story to run full circle. In my files, I have a list of 29 notable unsolved Yorkshire murders committed between 1903 and 1971. I prefer not to deal in the current and its still raw heartbreak. One of the most sensational and dramatic unsolved Yorkshire murders perpetrated, known also as the Moorcock Inn case or the Marsden Moor murders, is the tragic tale of a double murder at the lonely inn on Marsden Moor in 1832 in which several facts and clues seem to have a definite bearing on the resolution, but eventually come to nothing. The victims were 84-year-old William Bradbury, landlord of the inn (known as Bill o'Jacks) and his son Thomas, aged 46. They were shot following a massive struggle as Thomas was a giant of a man who was in the habit of throwing nuisance drinkers over the back wall. Bill, before he died, made the intriguing statement that 'Pat' or 'Pad' did the deed.

The complication comes in that there were Irish

workers nearby ('paddies') and local pedlars known as Burn Platters. A man named Reuben Platt had listened to the old man foolishly talk about his stash of money in the bar and he was suspected as was Red Bradbury, of a well-known local criminal family.

Red's brother Joe had been prosecuted for poaching by the Bradbury family who owned the pub (no relation) and was due to appear in court in Pontefract the day after the murder. Bill, living in such a rural spot and without immediate recourse to help, had foolishly bragged about his fear of banks and his habit of keeping money on the premises. There is no doubt that he was inviting trouble. The murder scene was horrendous. Poor Mary, the old man's granddaughter, walked in on a scene of carnage. A contemporary account, describes the murder scene: 'The confusion was indescribable. Not only was the furniture overturned and broken as if a tremendous struggle had taken place. Not only was blood spattered everywhere as if the combatants had passed, wrestling from room to room. The floor was torn up, the wall torn down. Cupboards were open and every particle of panelling was smashed. While upstairs, rifled drawers and mattresses slit from end to end lay piled in hideous confusion...'

Until the time that the Moorcock was pulled down in 1937, the murder and the surrounding area had been the subject of morbid tourism and local folklore, with ghost stories attached to the tale as well, as illustrated by the text on the tombstone of the victims in Saddleworth churchyard: 'Those who now talk of far-famed Greenfield's hills, will think of Bill o'Jacks and Tom' Bills, such interest did their tragic end excite, that 'ere they were removed from human sight, thousands on thousands daily came to see the bloody scene of the catastrophe.'

Writing Crime and the Fascination of Deviance

From time to time, interested parties looked again into the horrible events of that day, as in 1959 when the Saddleworth History Club resolved to investigate but they too hit a brick wall, as so often happens in the scrutiny of provincial cold cases.

The club, usually numbering 30 members, was swelled by new faces, and a hundred people crammed into the Church Inn, at Uppermill. The *Yorkshire Post* crime reporter was there as well, and he described the scene. 'It was a strange and fearful sight. The room was blacked out. Five candles and a couple of oil lamps provided the only light. Mr Clifford Buckley said, "The murderer is believed to have called here for a drink before he committed his foul crime. He may have been in this room we sit in tonight... When a dog started howling in the yard outside, the time seemed ripe for anything..."'

The obvious main suspect was Joe Bradbury, who was to appear in court in Pontefract the next day and was heard to say: 'Tom Bradbury will never appear against me!' He was subsequently acquitted. According to the *Yorkshire Post* at the time, 'Tom Bradbury, crossing his father's part of the moors one night caught Joe Bradbury in the act of poaching. It was an easy matter for the giant wrestler to carry the thief to the house, to lock him in a cupboard for a night, and the next morning to hand him over to the police. Joe was bound over to appear at the next assizes...'

Almost certainly Joe Bradbury did the deed but why did the dying words indicate the two groups of itinerant workers? The old man had spoken unwisely about his savings hidden somewhere in the inn and suspicion would naturally fall on the Irish at that time as they were blamed for anything of the slightest transgression. The popular press depicted Irish people as brutal, beast-like, muscular creatures of some sub-species. They were in England in their thousands, building the canals and later the railways and were strong, clannish, transitory and underpaid. All the ripest of ingredients for scapegoating.

2
•
FAMOUS HANGMEN
AND OTHER CHARACTERS

I was in the archives in Doncaster, sitting waiting for a musty old file of papers to be found and handed over, as I have done so often. Over the years, working with paper sources for looking into the past, I've had everything that could be imagined in the bundles that arrive on the desk. There has been earth, dried blood, mysterious dark stains, doodles from famous villains, notebooks with unfinished sentences and, strangest of all, a love poem written by an infamous villain, tucked away in a stack of yellowing correspondence.

When the latest package was presented, I couldn't believe what was hidden amongst it, a notebook with some jottings in pencil from a noted hangman named – Steve Wade. There is an accompanying photograph, a man with a drink and a cigarette, the face suggesting someone under pressure, maybe a nervous type. He was in office from 1941 to 1955 and had to retire through ill-health. He died in 1956, having been assistant to both Tom and Albert Pierrepoint. Steve handled 29 hangings as chief executioner and was also in the transport business, running buses. When he wrote to the Home Office to offer his services as a hangman, he was at first refused as he was too young but Wade was determined because he eventually wrote again and was placed on a waiting list and given instruction before being appointed deputy to Thomas Pierrepoint.

When I first saw him I thought, with a shiver, that he might be related. He had a look of some of the men in my branch of Wades. But investigating family history brought no links.

The other Steve Wade went to live in Doncaster in 1935 and he established his coaching business in the Waterdale area. His first formal job as assistant hangman was with Tom Pierrepoint at Wandsworth, where they strung up George Armstrong who had spied for Germany. Armstrong was tried at the Old Bailey, then appealed and after that failed, found himself facing the noose. Before he began his work in Yorkshire in earnest, Wade aided Albert hanging another spy, the notorious execution of the Karel Richter which was something of an ordeal. Richter's records have now been released and we know that his mission was to deliver funds and a spare wireless crystal to another spy. He was given a code and money and also a supply of secret ink and was even briefed on what to say if interrogated. According to some opinions, his arrival on espionage work was part of a 'double-cross 'system which meant that agents were captured and given an option either to work as double agents or to face the gallows.

Richter was parachuted into Hertfordshire in 1941 and,

according to MI5, landed on the 14th May and was caught by war reserve constable Boott at London Colney talking to a lorry driver who turned out to be the spy. Richter was taken to Fleetville Police Station and there he showed a Czech passport. When searched he had a ration book, compass, cash and a map of East Anglia. Photographs survive of Richter with army and police going back to a field to find his buried equipment. He stands in one pointing whilst surrounded by various personnel. He was destined to be Pierrepoint and Wade's client on 10th December, 1941.

Wade kept notes on what happened that day. It was an horrendous experience for the young hangman so early in his career.

First he wrote, 'Karl Richter, 29, five feet and eleven and a half inches. 172 lbs. Execution: good under the circumstances.' However, that turns out to be something of an understatement. Richter, a marine engineer, was athletic, strong and determined to cause the maximum resistance when the hangmen arrived at the death-cell. Wade wrote: 'On entering cell to take prisoner over and pinion him he made a bolt towards the door. I warded him off and he then charged the wall at a terrific force with his head. This made him most violent. We seized him and strapped his arms at rear…. The belt was faulty, not enough eyelid holes, and he broke away from them. I shouted to Albert 'He is loose' and he was held by warders until we made him secure. He could not take it and charged again for the wall screaming HELP ME.'

Even at the scaffold, Richter fought: '… he then tried to get to the opposite wall over trap. Legs splayed. I drew them together and see Albert going to the lever. I shout wait, strap on legs and down he goes. As rope was fixed around his neck he shook his head and the safety ring, too big, slips……' Wade's notes have a tone of relief as he writes finally: 'Neck broken immediately.' At the end of them he wrote that he said something to Albert, a comment along the lines of 'I would not miss this for fifty pounds...' Nigel West, in his history of MI5, has an addendum to add to Steve Wade's terrible memoir. 'The grisly scene had a profound effect on all those present, and, indirectly, on some other Abwehr agents. Several months later Pierrepoint and his chief assistant, Steve Wade, carried out an execution at Mountjoy in Dublin. News of Richter's final moments reached Gunther Schutz and his fellow internees... Irish warders gleefully recounted the details of the struggle on the scaffold, sending Richter's former colleagues into a deep depression.'

Wade's last hanging was a more straightforward case, that of a man killing his wife's mother, the woman who he believed stood in the way of his happiness with Maureen Farrell of Wombwell.

Her mother, Clara, became an object of hatred for the young man, Alec Wilkinson, only 22-years-old. On 1st May, 1955, Wilkinson had a great deal to drink and worked himself up to a mood of extreme violence and enmity towards Clara Farrell. Not long after their marriage, Alec and Maureen had been under pressure and the relationship between Alec and his mother-in-law was one of extreme tension; she apparently always criticising him and making it clear that he was worthless. On the fateful day when he walked up to the front door of the Farrell's home nearby, he had a burning spite in him and was in a mood to use it. First he sprang on Clara and punched her and then slammed her head on the floor. Such was Wilkinson's fury, that he went for a knife in the kitchen, stabbed her, and then did something that suggests a psychosis as well as a drunken fit; he piled furniture on the woman and set fire to it. Wilkinson left as someone came to try to put out the fire but later confessed and one of his statements was that he was not sorry for what he had done. There was an attempt to demonstrate provocation and even a petition to save him, but Wilkinson was found guilty of murder at Sheffield and sentenced to hang.

Afterwards, Steve Wade returned to Doncaster and lived on Thorne Road, Edenthorpe. He had been a café proprietor as well as operating Wade's Motor Coaches. He retired in 1955 and died just over a year after hanging Wilkinson, on 22 December, 1956, at Doncaster Royal Infirmary. His official obituary contained the note: 'Buried at Rosehill Cemetery (unconsecrated) in Doncaster.' He seems to have been a very reticent character. Syd Dernley, who worked with him, said simply: 'Wade was a quiet man and said no more than hello when introduced.' Laconic Albert Pierrepoint noted of Wade in his autobiography, *Executioner: Pierrepoint*, that he was: 'A good, reliable man.'

In 1973 I started my studies, with five other students, for a master's degree in Dialectology at the University of Leeds. Each week we met in the study of the amazing Stanley Ellis, an expert in phonetics. With hours spent in the language laboratories too, I never realized then how useful such knowledge could be in forensics. But the whole world was soon to find out when quiet, reserved, unassuming Stanley was to be centrally involved in the most high-profile crime investigation that Yorkshire had known. In the mid to late 1970s, the county was gripped in fear by the mass crimes of the Yorkshire Ripper. With genuine leads precious, a tape arrived at Police Headquarters in Millgarth, Leeds.

The taunting recording, goaded the police chiefs into believing that they were closer to catching their man. What they needed to know was where did the speaker come from?

Not just that he was vaguely a 'Geordie' but where exactly. My tutor, Stanley Ellis – an expert in linguistic boundaries - and Jack Windsor Davies got to work on the voice of 'Wearside Jack.' He pinpointed the speaker, who tormented detective George Oldfield, to the former pit village of Castletown, Sunderland.

Subsequent investigative work in the area proved the sender to be a hoax. But what it showed was that, like a fingerprint, we each have an idiolect; a very specific voice print, unique to our intonation patterns. Stanley was the ideal tutor, approachable, chatty, full of anecdotes and advice, but never overbearing and always ready to listen. I had no idea at the time that he might be dashing off after a tutorial to give expert testimony in a Crown Court anywhere in the land. He was a trail-blazer in a new science with an exciting career trajectory.

When PC Ian Broadhurst was shot and killed near Dib Lane in Leeds in December, 2003, the accused was brought to trial and the jury heard recordings of a 'Nathan Coleman' placing bets on the phone. Dr John French was able to show that 'Coleman' and the man in the dock, David Bieber, were one and the same. Canadian Bieber had been in West Yorkshire some time and the phonetic mix of those two components gave him distinctive features. Dr French concluded that the chances of the two voices being different to be, 'very remote.' Fingerprint evidence backed this up too, and Bieber was convicted of murder. It was a case that came close to me. The murder was where I used to deliver milk back in the sixties. My father, working for the Leeds Co-operative Society, recharged his milk-barrow just a hundred yards from where P.C. Broadhurst died. I, feeling a personal need, wanted his killer caught and locked up. Linguistic science had sorted it.

Another encounter which opened up a new angle on a notorious crime happened when I walked into my local library. At the issuing desk was Sandra and we started to chat about our interest in crime writing. She has a good stock of scrap-books about her involvement in one of the major enquiries in the history of crime, the Moors Murders, which took place on the border between the white and red rose counties. She was secretary for Bob Talbot and a team of detectives who investigated the case and, as we looked through them, she pointed out locations in and around Saddleworth and talked about a woman detective she knew on the case, so that I felt as if I was back at the time and scene. It was a rare chance to talk about a period in modern history when police work was just emerging from its blue lamp image and was being given to us as something close to a more modern science. She played a central role in the media show as the tabloids struggled to find ways of extracting daily stories while the force was out combing the moors, then going on to join the force. She often used the word camaraderie, explained that there was always a professional respect and that teamwork was at the core of everything.

The Moors case, with its lingering 'Jack the Ripper' fascination for that generation, is a fascinating chapter in the annals of modern police work. It was a steady, regular and ordered enquiry, with meticulous monitoring and recording. In a pre-computer age, the office work functioned around phone calls, record cards and a coded range of knocks on the office wall: one for tea, two for a useful communication and three for 'get out there now!' The days of the enquiry were long and hard, Sandra being collected at eight-thirty in the morning, taken to the office in Hyde, and then work progressing steadily right through to eight at night. The journalists and writers flocked to her office. She met Emlyn

Williams, the author of the first book on the case, *Beyond Belief*, and she and a friend were dogged by reporters and they sometimes had to hide. The whole business became so farcical that one day a newspaperman came into her office pretending to be ill. His performance was worthy of Olivier, but transparently a sham. She had to fuss and seem concerned, while all the time watching him like a hawk. There is nothing sensational in her memories of the time. It was, she told me: 'Just careful, routine work, as with any case...we had no idea at the time that this was to be momentous and in so many books.' She recalls the conversations she had with Myra Hindley without a hint of salaciousness and the times when Ian Brady was left in the room behind hers.

Brady and Hindley quickly realised that they had a mutual relish for sadism. Brady was interested in Nazi ideologies as well, and when the couple went to live with Hindley's grandmother in Hattersley, Lancashire, Brady began to enjoy showing off his twisted imagination and love of weaponry to Hindley's young brother-in-law, David Smith. Crimes were talked about and became reality one day when Brady brought home a teenager called Edward Evans. Hindley went to fetch Smith and when he arrived at their place he watched Evans being murdered with an axe. Smith called the police, the body was found and the search for the killers began. Suitcases were discovered in a left luggage store with weapons, tape recordings and other papers inside. Tapes and other materials made it clear that two missing children, Lesley Ann Downey and John Kilbride, had also been killed. Photos of the two killers out on Saddleworth Moor led police to the burial places, and the couple were arrested and tried at Chester Crown court, being convicted in May, 1966 and sentenced to life imprisonment. There is no substitute for a writer than the information gleaned from a witness to or a participant in a crime. But it is not the notoriety of the case, it is the human interest material that really attracts.

I've also always had a fascination with the history and work of provincial detectives. The Bow Street Runners had initially dealt with cases across the country, along with agents provocateurs, who had come north to mix with Chartists and Luddites during the years of radical activism in the early nineteenth century. But from around 1850, provincial detective forces were created, particularly after the Fenian bombings and Manchester Fenian murders of the 1850s and '60s. One notable character in this respect operated around Doncaster and Sheffield: a man called George Winn. Following the accepted practice, he had a string of contacts and snitches, used plain clothes disguises and was exceptionally vigilant. Those in the role also had to learn how to uncover the more subtle types of crime, the non-violent ones that involved swindles, frauds and deception. In 1858 Winn found himself on the trail of a forger who worked across South Yorkshire, going to horse fairs and passing dud cheques and counterfeit notes. He had the same name as another very famous man of Victorian times – artisit William Morris – and was caught courtesy of the *Police Gazette*.

This publication, still going today, was originally called *Hue and Cry,* and was circulated across London at first and then further afield, with descriptions of wanted criminals, lists of army deserters and short accounts of crimes.

In April 1858, Detective Wetherall of Sheffield was on the hunt for Morris and when he went into one of the public houses where villains tended to congregate, he saw a copy of the magazine on a table. The publication was folded with a line drawing of Morris, visible. Wetherall deduced that Morris, through sheer crook's vanity, had wanted to see how he was described in print and it didn't take long to find out that Morris was indeed lodging in a room upstairs and was in it at that moment.

Thirty years before, passing false bank notes had been a hanging offence and even in the 1850s it had a likely sentence of multiple years of penal servitude. In those days when police communication was still with whistles or feet, Wetherall had to run to the nearest police station for help. He went in search of Winn and the two detectives returned to Morris's room, Wetherall identified him and Winn at once seized him. The two detectives saw that Morris had tried to drop a parcel in the corner of the room and, when they retrieved it, they found a roll of forged notes. Morris also had a bag of forged sovereigns on him, called 'jacks,' the capture was a major breakthrough.

Also in Sheffield, Winn's reputation was further enhanced when he collared a man who had been around Doncaster and called at a butcher's saying he had several 'fat beasts' for sale at below half the accepted price. Winn learned that from a contact that the man was to gather his animals in the Sheffield Shambles and sell them there, went in plain clothes, made the arrest and had the cattle taken to the Yellow Lion. In 1864 he was involved in one of his most high-profile cases and one of Doncaster's largest scale burglaries in the nineteenth century. The crooks were George Harris and George Perry from Huddersfield and they travelled across Yorkshire, casing likely targets for robbery and then worked as a team. On the 12th September, the pair loitered on Christchurch Terrace by a house owned by a Miss Drabwell. She had gone away for a while to stay with her niece and on the 20th the police were told that there had been, 'an extensive burglary' there. The thieves had broken into the house from the rear and then worked recklessly through the place, ransacking everything. Miss Drabwell was wealthy and kept a wine cellar. Police found that several bottles had been drunk, along with two bottles of brandy and the burglars had also smoked cigars. As to the booty the crooks went away with, the extensive heist included; silver spoons, candlesticks, a silk mantle, silk jackets, a cashmere tablecloth and all kinds of other silver items. They had also taken 30 yards of satin and all manner of jewellery. Their likely 'fence' was a certain Charles Walker and detectives kept an eye on him. Sure enough, at a shop belonging to, ironically, a Mr Cash in Sheffield, a man who was working with the burglars went in and offered two seals. They had a crest on them and Cash was suspicious and asked the man to come back with more items and he would by them as a job lot. But he also told the police and George Winn was waiting for the perpetrators. Walker came to the shop with the burglars behind and had a bag under his coat. Winn grabbed him, Harris and Perry ran off, but Walker spilled the beans under interrogation and led Winn and officers to the lodging house where all the stolen goods were kept. The success of the hunt for the Doncaster burglars was the beginning of the burgeoning Yorkshire detective network. The pair returned to Huddersfield but descriptions had been sent on and police were waiting for them. They were in the dock at Doncaster police court soon after and then sent on to Leeds Assizes and a long time behind bars.

When any kind of new or refurbished pub or 'eating house' was established, it was checked out. Known criminals would often be looking for a fresh den with a legitimate front. Winn was often the man called in to investigate places like the Alexandra Music Hall in Sheffield, which required a licence to import foreign wines. The magistrates sent him to check them out and make sure the operation was legitimate.

The new detectives in the shires were powerful, influential men in areas of urban life, dealing with both the physical side of policing and with newer white collar crime as society expanded and industry diversified.

In complete contrast, Charlie Peace's life and crimes dominated the history of Yorkshire villains until the advent of the Yorkshire Ripper. When he was finally executed at Armley Gaol, there was a main feature in *The Illustrated Police News*, showing the Lincolnshire hangman, William Marwood, at work in the execution suite and Charlie on his knees. His villainy merited a full volume in the prestigious Notable Trials series published by Hodge of Edinburgh, alongside such as Crippen and Ronald True. All the aspects of his story invoke legend, folk tale and an element of the grotesque; everything about his life was unusual. He was born in 1832, the son of a one-legged lion tamer, John Peace, and by the age of 12 was working in a rolling mill at Millsands. It was a fearful accident there, when a red hot bar impaled him in the leg, which led to the first stage of his fearsome and ill-formed appearance. Peace earned a living afterwards playing the violin and starting a career of petty crime. A lawyer writing in 1906 noted: 'He was in great demand at concerts... On one occasion he had an engagement at a theatre and was billed as The Modern Paganini... His performance consisted of playing on a single string.' In 1876, he was in Manchester and killed a policeman. Another man, William Habron, was tried and convicted and Peace attended the trial, later saying he had enjoyed the spectacle.

He began to harass and trail a Mrs Katherine Dyson, the wife of an engineer he had got to know. He became such a threatening nuisance that the Dysons moved house but Peace followed them and one night, as her husband went to an outside toilet, Peace was there with a gun. When Dyson came out, Peace said: 'I'm here to annoy you, and I'll annoy you wherever you go,' shooting him through the head. He then moved to London and began a new life, living as John Ward. He put up a front of being an amateur businessman and inventor but at night he was still doing burglaries. He shot and wounded a police officer one night while being chased during a robbery. It was when his mistress, Susan Ward, informed on him that the law finally caught up with him. In 1876 he left Doncaster to live in lodgings with his mistress in Hull, where they were known as Mr and Mrs Thompson. It seems that at times Charlie did help to run the pie shop they inhabited but he couldn't resist some thievery and went out on burglary trips, on one night doing seven houses. One biography of him claims that he shot a bullet into the ceiling of one house, and was disturbed having his fun when the residents came home in another. One writer claims that the law came hunting for Charlie at his home and that he hid behind a chimney on the roof.

Once caught, Peace tried a daring escape. He was being escorted to Leeds to stand trial for the Yorkshire murder and asked permission to urinate which entailed doing so through an open carriage window. He dived out, kicked one foot free and hung from the window. An officer in the escort tried to restrain him but Peace lacerated his arm. Unable to fully free himself and severely injured, Peace was reinterned and brought to trial, proved to be the man who killed Arthur Dyson and sentenced to hang. He may have been responsible for more murders, at Banner Cross and Whalley Edge, Manchester.

He was hanged by Marwood on 25th February, 1879. The papers were still full of the stunning achievement of the soldiers at Rorke's Drift in the Zulu War, but Peace's death made the headlines. To the very end, Peace was a character.

He joked: 'I wonder if the hangman can cure my sore throat!' Being a man with a sense of drama, he insisted on a last speech for the sake of the reporters. He said: 'Say my last wishes and my last respects are to me children and their dear mother. I hope that no person will disgrace himself by taunting them or jeering them... Oh My Lord have mercy on me!' According to Marwood: 'He was such a desperate man but passed away like a summer's eve.'

It became a Victorian narrative image of renown, so much so that Madame Tussauds created a tableaux from the scene. In 1929, there was a show at the Ambassador's Theatre in London called *The Misdoings of Charlie Peace* such was the fascination with the man. It was billed as: 'A report in sixteen instalments of the life of Charlie Peace between August 1st 1876 when he was working as a framer and gilder... to the condemned cell in Armley Gaol.'

3
•
GROWING UP
IN DARK LEEDS

I remember the scene very well. It lodges in my mind like a freeze-frame of some grim art movie. It was in the back room of a Leeds bakery. My father worked there and he was mainly at the counter, although he did help out with the bread-baking at times. I was waiting for him to finish doing the delivery orders and his boss chatted to me in this back room. Suddenly he asked me: 'Do you know how to hold a knife then, young Stephen?'

I shook my head. He took grip on a long, sharp carver swung it a little, then lifted it high and brought it down hard, cutting into the side of a thick wooden board. I jumped slightly but tried not to show any fear. I thought he was about to do that trick where the blade is stuck between the fingers. 'That's how you use a blade, see?' he told me. 'You show it who's the gaffer! Right?' I nodded again. He asked me to have a go, to do the same thing. I didn't fancy it and hoped my dad would come soon. 'Anyway, watch how I hold it... see where the fingers are? Now I can rock it back and forth.... in command you see?' It seemed like hours before my dad came and we went home.

When he did come to fetch me, my dad said I was very quiet. I just asked: 'Is Mr Morris sick?' To which he replied: 'No... he's fine. Why?' Dad was concerned. 'Nothing. Just me being daft!' I said, and switched to talk about Leeds United's form. But that scene has never left me. There was something about the man's affection for cutting and slicing that is lodged as a reminder that man and weapon have a bond, an affiliation, and that handles, stocks, blades and barrels are not simply tools, they are an extension of a certain human will. Later, I was also to meet guys who had knife and bullet wounds to show me, usually with a wry smile. Whenever I saw a scar from such a wound, I recalled that neat, snug union of metal and human flesh.

In 1948, when I made my appearance in the world, the effects of the War were still seeping into every crack in life like a dark, corrosive liquid. There was, as I grew up, a feeling that the adults around the place had all seen terrible privation and suffering. There was uncle Bill Schofield, who told us about seeing Mussolini and his woman strung up. There were weapons from the conflict everywhere. Uncle Bill Longfellow had his Chindit hat and a kukri knife. There always seemed to be warnings of a dark and unsafe world outside the family. Looking back, Leeds was a place where there was a certain level of feral amorality around me when I went to secondary school at Osmondthorpe, half a mile from the junction of Selby Road and York Road – where one leads to Cross Gates and the other to Halton and Garforth. Matters came nearer home when the family grapevine communicated some bad news – one of my cousins was in prison.

Throughout childhood, there had always been the threat of a punishment involving being sent to 'an approved school.' Anyone who repeatedly crossed the behaviour line was likely to be dispatched to this mysterious institution by cloaked and mortar-boarded headmaster, Mr Paterson. What happened to 'bad lads' was never specifically described, but the very thought of the waiting punishment was enough to instil extreme fear. Many lads at school had big brothers and the culture was one of bullying, intimidation and threats. Every break-time, the pupils would spill out into the vast, sloping playground and there would be pecking-order fights. Sometimes, the violence that bubbled and simmered broke out into a large-scale confrontation, exemplified the day that a Teds gang arrived at the gate, swinging bike-chains and rattling knives on the railings. Their leader shouted out for: 'That twat who teaches science.' Apparently, his little brother had been caned, and that was done after the science teacher sent him to the Head. It was a dinner time but play stopped as the chunky Maths teacher, Mr Wilson, led out the battalion of teachers and there, before all the boys, was a battle royal.

It seems, from research done by Michael Macilwee, that the Teds were late on the scene in Leeds. Their heyday was in the early fifties and this fight took place around '59. Leeds had never been as prominent a place for them as Bradford. There were several gangs there and on one occasion in 1955 a notorious scrap took place between them and the police near the Ideal Ballroom in Bankfoot. There had been a warning of trouble and a van full of coppers was ready to intervene. The result was a very violent skirmish and three young women were stabbed. Three Teds had prison terms imposed. Macilwee noted in his account of the phenomenon, there were several Ted gangs in Bradford – the Mambo Boys, the Abbey Mob and the Mau Mau.

For much of my childhood, although my family and home were safe, there was still a universal sense of deviance and knowledge that the villains were out there. They were referred to as 'bad 'uns.' My dad, who didn't read books, relied on his Sunday papers, the *News of the World* and *The People*. They inherited the obsessions of the old penny dreadful. Consequently, Sunday was run through with gory headlines such as 'Ladykiller on the Run' or 'Man slain outside his local.' They led you to believe that every poorly-lit street was a potential murder scene. Any solitary walk in Leeds after dark meant a frisson of apprehension. When Hammer horror films came along in the sixties they confirmed the feeling that the supposed rational mind was always under threat from the forces of darkness.

There was a typically unnerving incident still in the air too, the Halifax Slasher Case. It had happened just before the war, in 1938. A mysterious figure skulked around in the dark, accosting folk and slashing out at them with a razor before disappearing into the night. Scotland Yard were called in and there was a long list of victims, including a man in Elland who was attacked in his shop and a woman at Dean Clough Mill who had come face to face with the Slasher. It rapidly became clear, however, that there was no such person, it was a moral panic. People ended up in court. Five were indicted at Halifax quarter sessions with causing a public mischief. One law report, at appeal, commented: 'These cases are of interest both by reason of the unusual circumstances in which the offences were committed, the state of alarm created among the population of Halifax... and the technical defect in the caution administered by the police officer...' But such is the nature of fear. When I was eight, this world of shady transgression stood in front of me, represented by a burly individual loitering outside the Corn Exchange in Leeds. He thought I was alone, stepped out, fixed himself in my way and grabbed my arm. He said: 'Now lad, I've summat for you!' He took something out of his pocket, and before I could see what it was, my father had come up behind him and the man disappeared into the shadows.

Then there was Armley gaol, that brooding presence, like a great threat over the city. The magnificent but forbidding sight of the castellated features has the reputation of being a harsh regime. The cells have housed many of the most notorious villains in history although gone are the death suite and scaffold. It opened in 1847 on the penitentiary model, radial wings from a central tower. At first, as the plans for the design show, there were to be separate areas for women and children, including cells and exercise yards. In that massive place there have been murderers, robbers, bombers, psychopaths, gangland leaders and criminally insane types; women under mental duress who have killed their babies, and even the less violent but more deviously cunning plotters and forgers of the underworld.

Many of the early hangmen there were people with drink problems. One such was Thomas Askern of York. Typical of his actions was the execution of the Sheffield killers, Myers and Sargisson. So desperate was Myers to avoid the noose that he slit his own throat but the dictates of the law had to be followed and if a man was to hang, then hang he would. He was stitched up and the two men were paraded in the only public execution to be outside the prison (they ended in 1868). Myers died quickly but Sargisson took several minutes as he struggled on the end of the rope. Grotesquely, the slit throat of Myers bled profusely and the corpse was soaked in blood.

Murder in Mind

There were plenty more Armley hangings but perhaps few so emotionally complex and harrowing as the double execution of a couple who had murdered the woman's husband. Wife and lover died together, but it was the hanging of the woman that affected the hangman, John Ellis, very deeply. On the day they swung, Emily Swann had said to her lover: 'Good morning John,' and the man who had beaten her husband to death replied quietly: 'Good morning love.' Ellis wrote in his memoirs: 'She was 42 years old, a little stumpy, round-faced woman, only four feet 10 inches tall and 122 pounds in weight. She was the first condemned woman I had ever seen, and frankly I didn't think the authorities would allow her to go to the scaffold.' But they did. Ellis, when he heard the last conversation between the two condemned, reflected: 'This, I had to confess, was an astonishing scene, a dialogue between two people, one a woman, standing with pinioned arms and legs, faces blotted out by shapeless white bags and with ropes fixed around their necks.'

In 1958, two dangerous characters escaped from Armley in the night. Michael Millard and Royal Pettinger managed to force the bars on their cell window and somehow got out of the grounds, presumably over the wall. A third man was captured. Four years later, a prison officer from Armley was attacked in Huddersfield. He was found on open ground having been beaten up after a car stopped and pulled him inside. The jail was designed as a fortress. The oldest part still has the radial four wings and it covers around eight hectares. When it first opened it boasted 334 cells. Today, as part of the modern prison service, it includes such things as a gymnasium, healthcare, help with drug problems, a chaplaincy and all kinds of support for prisoners and their families. The Victorian inmates, with their long hours of physical labour and thin gruel, would not recognise the place, despite the modern privations of overcrowding. The main purpose behind a Victorian prison was that it should remake the offender by means of the 'dignity of work,' with ample time for remorse and repentance. The prisoner's routine, included such as making sacks, gardening, working with oakum, tailoring or cooking, together with periods of time devoted to reflection of their evil.

The last person to be hanged at Armley was Zsiga Pankotia in June, 1961. He killed Eli Myers in Chelwood Avenue, off Street Lane in Leeds, his market trader victim being a man who had foolishly bragged about the money he had won on the football pools. Pankotia broke into Myers's home with the intention of merely stealing something, but Myers disturbed him and Pankotia took hold of a bread knife. A desperate struggle then began as Myers took on the intruder; Myers was stabbed to death and Pankotia drove away in his van. It was to be a complex case because Myers had a heart condition, confirmed by the famous Dr. Poulson of Leeds University. The issue became, was Myers killed or did his weak heart fail in the fight? The jury found Pankotia guilty and he was the last client of Mr Harry Allen, hangman, at Armley.

Gunther Fritz Edwin Podola was the last man executed in Britain for killing a police officer. That was in 1959 and I was eleven. The name was exotic, alien. It registered like something from a film. His name lodged in my imagination, as did the sad tale of a woman who longed for company and paid the ultimate price for trust. It happened just yards from where I first walked to work.

Mary Judge was well-known around the area of Kirkgate, between Leeds Parish Church and the Regent Hotel. It is a few streets of dark alleys, not far from the Calls – notoriously unsafe places for walks by night 40 years ago.

But Mary, 40-years-old and a cheery, sociable soul, liked a drink and preferred that area in and under the railway arches. It was then a desolate place. I often walked past and saw gatherings of tramps, drunks and the raucous around that viaduct. At the same time, I saw similar groups gathered outside St George's Crypt and up towards Park Lane as I went to college there. Looking back, was Mary, I wondered when I first considered the case, a victim, simply at random, from inside this whirlpool of violence and hatred? She was discovered at just before midnight by a passer-by on 22nd February 1968, battered and mostly naked, with her clothes scattered around her body. She was only five feet five, with brown hair, and had been wearing a quite garish outfit, definitely not colour-co-ordinated, so that would have made her noticeable. Her skirt was dark blue; the shoes green; white blouse, and her coat was a black check. She had severe head injuries.

The area was sealed off and arc-lights set up. She was well known to the barmen of the pubs around there, such as the Brougham and the Regent. People said she was: 'Always friendly and happy, liked a drink, and loved to stop and talk to children.' The patch of land is close to the Leeds central bus station, and at that time the area was notorious for its attraction to beggars and tramps who would often cadge money along the bus station platforms. By day it was busy, there was a huge Pilkington's Glass office nearby and commuter crowds would walk from the buses past the abattoir to Vicar Lane. By night, the area was well frequented by prostitutes. Whether Mary was on the game is not clear. She lived in East End Park, on Glendale Street, a long walk up towards the Shaftesbury cinema along the York Road. If she was a familiar figure down by the buses, she needed a good reason to walk more than a mile down to the pubs she liked – and alone. But Mary's murder had added fascination and drama to it, people saw her being attacked. That was because the Hull train rattled past the Parish Church at 10.18 that night, and several passengers on it saw the assailant. A small boy was the main witness. He came forward with his mother and gave a description of a tall man of slim build, with long dark hair and wearing a dark suit. The train passed within a mere 50 yards of the patch of grass where the killing happened. Mary had also been seen outside the Regent Hotel earlier that night and it also became obvious that the killer would have had plenty of her blood on his clothes. Appeals were made to local dry-cleaners to be vigilant but nothing came of that, so the train sightings became the main leads.

A reconstruction was staged. Officers boarded a train at Cross Gates and PC Eileen Playforth took the part of poor Mary Judge. It took just 15 seconds for the train to pass the scene; it was winter, late at night. But one positive element emerged, a man was seen leaving the scene by a Bradford commuter, also on that Hull train. At that point on the journey, passing quite high on the viaduct over the patch of grass, the view would have been quite distorted. But there was enough seen to make a helpful descriptive statement. Yet all this work and methodical investigation brought no positive result. The crime remains a cold case.

Of all the unsolved murders in Leeds, this one reaches deeply into the atmosphere of the Leeds streets in the late '60s. There was something in the air then, a sense of liberation after the austerities of the decade before. People did socialise more around town but some areas were 'no go.' Her openness to others made Mary very vulnerable. At one time some writers thought that she might even have been an early Yorkshire Ripper victim but that is now unsupported. All we are left with is another Leeds mystery.

Murder in Mind

When I left school, without qualifications, I still had the lust for learning in me, and as well as working at evening classes for GCE certificates, I used Leeds Central Library every week, making use of its wonderful collection of LPs of Shakespeare. They had a full set of the recordings made by the Marlowe Society and other groups, and that is how I first began to relish Shakespeare's stories, especially the historical plays. One day, in the entrance to the library, there was an exhibition put on by the Richard III Society, Yorkshire branch, and I joined. I went along to their next meeting, in a terrace house beside Headingley cricket ground, and there I met a man who was to be a profound influence on my writing, Arthur Cockerill, a Leeds teacher and actor. On that evening, after just a few introductions, there in front of me was the funeral cortege scene from *Richard III* with Arthur and an actress called Claire Routh. It was magical, entrancing. There was evil, acted out with a trickle of insights into deviousness and obnoxious seduction.

It was in that sitting-room, looking at this bohemian world that existed in a Leeds suburb, so different from my own working-class background, that I saw the effects of our concerns with truth and transgression. Later, as a student having to write essays on the literary Richard III, it helped me to look for the truth.

4

•

REVISITING MY FAVOURITE YORKSHIRE TALES

In early 2016, the news on the radio informed me that there had been a 14 per cent increase in homicide over the last year. In a work published in 1964, *A Calendar of Murder*, the authors list, 'thumb-nail sketches of every accused and victim' between 1957 and 1962. It seems that the propensity to take life, even if most killings are opportunist and not pre-meditated, has always been prevalent.

The more murder cases I looked in to, the more I felt distant from those individuals who committed such crimes. Later I met dozens of killers and worked with them on writing projects. I was introduced to some notorious ones but, mostly, those I came to know had taken the life of someone they knew or had committed the act while drunk or under the influence of drugs. Often, the reality of what they had done was very slow-burn. One man who came into prison had killed his wife and I was asked to talk to him just a day after his arrival on the wing. He had had his soul drawn out of him. He had been a husband and a worker, a father and a brother. Now he was a killer.

Sitting in a library studying a book of law and sucking on the end of a pencil, I once came across a renowned double killer, another who wore overalls and looked dreamy and subdued, ordinary. How does a writer or crime investigator get inside their chilling minds? In my years of delving into Yorkshire crime, there have been a select group of cases which represent the sheer fascination of an incomprehensible narrative. This chapter looks at them again and offers some revisionist thinking. The first is from Bradford.

It is the curious tale of Israel Blum and his journey from there to the Wirral, where he appears to have had an appointment with death. I had the basic details from Marie Campbell's *Curious Tales of Old West Yorkshire* (1999). The most detailed first account was back at the time of the disappearance in 1866 and printed in the *Keighley News*. Blum was second master at Bradford High School and was said to live a regular, disciplined life, being a reliable and morally upright member of the school community. On the day he travelled out of town, never to be seen again alive by anyone who knew him. He had taught in the morning as usual and then talked with another member of staff before rushing off. We know that he bought a copy of Charles Dickens' *David Copperfield* at Byles bookshop and then went to the Midland Station. On that occasion, though, he lied to his colleague Anderson, claiming he was planning to do some scientific work at home, whereas he was really dashing to catch a train out of the city. So begins the first set of questions in this mystery. Who was he planning to meet, and why?

Blum's body was found at Hoylake, close to the Mersey

estuary. A doctor and a constable made statements and the newspaper report stated that he was drenched on a rock, more or less in the foetal position. 'The face was calm, as if in sleep,' it said. His throat had been cut with two slashes and his copy of David Copperfield was found that evening by a man at Redstones, turned down at page 101. The initial inquest decided on a verdict of suicide but some medical opinion disagreed, notably that of Dr. Dodd from Hoylake, who suspected foul play. When, eventually, friends and colleagues travelled to Liverpool to confirm his identity, they also insisted that suicide was an impossible cause of death. Robbery was a motive because he left home with a significant of cash, around £16, and the body had only a few shillings on it. His watch and gold Albert chain were also missing. But, if it were murder following a theft, why were there still valuables on the body? More intriguingly, why was his body wet through when there had been no high tide?

Blum was engaged to a young woman who was living in London and a letter to her was uncovered in his jacket, written in April, a few weeks before he left Bradford. 'I had a strange letter from Leeds from a stranger who is staying here on business,' it read. 'He comes from Hamburg and wishes to see me. As it is impossible for me to go to Leeds until Saturday I must consider meanwhile what to do... a strange thing, is it not?' And the final part of the enigma was that the victim had a brother living in Hamburg who was known to be short of money, whose aim it was to emigrate to Australia and start a new life, but who had disappeared in Liverpool a few months before. He had previously visited Blum in Bradford for a loan.

Enquiries found witnesses around Hoylake, including a woman who had seen Blum alive at around eight in the evening standing on the beach near the Royal Hotel. Nothing collaborated the sighting and a request was made for a new enquiry. It was not held. Marie Campbell tried to follow up records of the case, claiming that there was a photograph of Blum's corpse and a print given to the Home Office, but there is no trace of it in the Public Records Office. Her writings also note that, 'a professional researcher has also been unsuccessful in locating information about Mr Israel James Blum in national repositories.' She points out interesting parallels between *David Copperfield* and the situation of Blum: a schoolmaster, an old school friend who dies in a storm at sea, a rich widow and close friend who goes to Australia.

Pure coincidence? Or a possible scenario that the man who wrote the letter had arranged a discreet meeting with Blum, mentioned the situation of his brother and was pressurising him to clear some of his sibling's debts. Another possibility is that the death was indeed related in some way to the content of the novel, acting out of a scenario perhaps shared by Blum and his assailant. Given that Dickens' story is partly about betrayal, a friendship that ends in disillusionment, and does so with imagery of the wild sea as a backdrop, it is worthy of further literary investigation, at least.

It is tempting to follow the line of thought connected to what was very much in vogue in the literature and culture of the 1850s: male friendship. Literary historians such as Carolyn Oulton noted that at that time: 'Romantic friendship, although largely inaccessible to modern ideals, enjoyed a high... cultural status in the nineteenth century. The form of friendship depended on both strong feelings and... startling rhetorical expression.' In other words, males could and did make grand, passionate and sometimes fantastical gestures regarding the closeness of the friendship. Oulton points out that David Copperfield has that kind of relationship with the 'bounder' Steerforth who, according to Oulton, 'Appropriates David's personal belongings and changes his name.'

Perhaps this is what was behind Blum's tryst. Page 101 is in a chapter called 'Enthusiasm' and the material there concerns the planned departure of the lovable wastrel, Wilkins Micawber, to take up a new life as a clerk to Uriah Heep in Canterbury. Like Blum, David first learns of this when he receives a letter which is an invitation to a celebratory gathering for dinner at Micawber's place. The other part of that chapter concerns a discussion of the return from India of Jack Maldon, that of a tutor and a former pupil, and it is about money. Teacher and student discuss some planned work on a dictionary – the tutor's lifelong project – and then Maldon and the tutor have an odd conversation when Maldon is asked if there is any news. He replies that the people in the North are always discontented and then says: 'There's a long statement in the papers, sir, about a murder... But somebody is always being murdered and I didn't read it.' When all the obvious lines of investigation are considered to be untenable, maybe, we are left with the uncanny link with the novel after all; death pact or unseemly killing, brother on brother, all for the cost of a ship abroad or away from debtors in pursuit. Blum's brother was his own imagined Steerforth, perhaps, and the teacher gave his life as well as his money for the dark alter ego he met that day near Hoylake. It is some narrative.

My first discoveries, as a crime writer, were about the initially shocking status of suicide as a crime. At first, all such courts were held with a jury but since 1927 they have only been needed in a few inquest cases; when the death has been in prison, in police custody, a case reportable by the Health and Safety Executive or in circumstances prejudicial to public safety. All that modern vocabulary would have been lost on the coroner for Leeds in the late Victorian and Edwardian period, John Cooper Malcolm. Malcolm was of Scottish origin but was born in the city. He was elected coroner in 1876 and held that office until 1923. He was the oldest in that position in England and saw every variety of death possible in the Leeds of the boom and bust years between the arrival of the new industries to the Great War and its aftermath.

A solicitor trained under the deputy to a former coroner, Malcolm was highly respected in his profession, so much so he was appointed president of the Coroners' Society of England and Wales. He had the particularly unpleasant duty of being coroner for Armley Gaol, holding 50 inquests on murderers there, including that of the famous Charlie Peace. Earlier inquests had been held in public houses and when he retired, Malcolm described these events. 'Publicans … were usually at great pains to make a coroner's jury comfortable, and the most that the innkeepers in Leeds got was a fee of five shillings for their trouble. Juries were made more comfortable than they sometimes are in vestries and school rooms where the inquests have been held since.'

Malcolm, a solid-looking man with a full beard and no-nonsense expression, was widowed twice and left a large fortune. He was described by a colleague as having: 'A cool, calm, judicious and judicial mind.' The deaths Malcolm had to handle were mostly those one might expect from the lives of people in a city undergoing huge social change; the pressures of hardship, unemployment, or conversely long and exhausting working hours. Moral problems, legal stresses and mental illness all became factors in the coroners' courts. Suicides were some of the commonest categories. Many were women who took their own lives because of problems relating to childbirth, prostitution or drink. A fairly typical case is that of Mary Ann Brooke, only 19-years-old, in 1885. She was the daughter of the manager of York Street Gasworks. Her mother reported at the inquest that the girl had been, 'Low and moody... though she had no reason to believe that she was insane,' as the *Yorkshire Post* reported. But what was much less common was the gruesome part of the tale, that at first a leg was found then later the rest of her. The police surgeon explained that the injuries were caused when she fell into the canal and hit something very hard. But all was not explained, her sister stated that Mary had in fact had mental problems and that her mind had been 'unhinged' for some time. The result was the one coroners dislike most, an open verdict, too many unanswered questions ruling out the definitive cause.

In 1856, James Foreman of Sussex Street, was a wood carver by profession who also acted as treasurer to a Friendly Society. The accounts did not balance and he clearly thought that fingers would point at him, leading to a state of mind so extremely distraught that he tried to cut his throat. His first attempt failed and he was watched closely thereafter, but one morning he walked into the office where his colleagues were working, blood spewing from him. He leaned over a basin and the blood from his throat filled it, the razor he'd used standing beside it. Deemed mentally unstable by the coroner, the saddest aspect – apart from the several children he left to suffer in the wake of his actions – was that the Society's funds were found to be perfectly in order and the books balanced.

Also quite common is this suicide from 1866, caused mainly by a gambling habit. Samuel Birchall worked for the Midland Railway for 20 years and was 55 at the time he took his own life. He was, as the local newspaper put it, 'Strongly addicted to the turf' and was of, 'Very dissipated habits.' He was quite a character, owning a shop as well as having a regular job, and houses in Sheffield and Leeds. On the fateful day, he was found clearly drunk and then heard to say that he was tired of the world. Then he admitted to his concerned family that he had, 'taken something.' It turned out to be sufficient opium to end his days despite doctors frantically trying to pump his stomach. The verdict was 'felo de se' - an important category of suicide, meaning self-murder and so a felony. As the death was before the 1870 Forfeiture Act, it meant that he legally lost all his goods and possessions. Sadly, that proved to be immaterial as he had gambled away virtually everything he possessed.

Some deaths have less obvious causes. John Rider of Briggate's body was found on a Tuesday morning in 1855 near the Bowling tunnel on the Lancashire to Yorkshire Railway. The corpse, lying across the rails, was terribly mutilated. His head and face had been dissected, a most distressing sight to those who first came across it, a man called Pearson alerting the police. He and a PC Womersly then had the unenviable task of gathering and transporting what was left of Mr Rider to the Queen Hotel. The inquest was in Wakefield, at the Royal Hotel and all that could be returned by way of a verdict was 'found dead.' The victim was only identified because of his distinctive clothing, including a cap made of dog-hair. The best the *Yorkshire Post* could offer was, 'No reason could be assigned for him doing this… except that the old man has for some time past manifested symptoms of dotage.'

John Malcolm also presided over a number of murders, as in the instance of the killing of John Manley by John Ross in 1881. Ross was seen to do the murder, in York Street, and there were witnesses, but they were friends of the killer. Ross arrived at The Railway Hotel, confronted Manley and said, openly: 'I have an old score to settle with you.' The killer, well known to the police, then escaped. At the inquest there was evidence from a range of people and nothing emerged that would have reduced the charge from murder to manslaughter.

Industrial accidents also formed a backbone of the coroner's work. Typical is the tale of poor Emma Pudson, aged just 16. She worked for Hinchcliffe's woollen mill on East Street as a sliver minder. The *Leeds Mercury* tells the awful events. 'About 12.30 on Saturday last she was engaged in partially cleaning three carders while the gearing was in motion, and while so occupied it would appear from the evidence, though no-one actually saw the accident, that her dress was caught by the machinery, and she was thrown with violence to the floor... She did not survive many minutes...'

Everything concerned with coroners' duties and courts' functions was contained in the standard text, Jervis on Coroners. Those elected had to be financially sound; could not be aldermen or councillors, and they had to live within the electoral district. They also had to be unrelated to any specific party or to any source of patronage.

In Georgian times, when crime and punishment were more rough and ready and open to many abuses, heart-rending infanticide was common. Often the cause was shame, as an illegitimate child created a massive and stressful social stigma not only for the mother, but the whole family. Hence we have horror stories of young women being sent to asylums, or more commonly, a trip to 'an aunt in the country' to 'take care of matters.' There were also economic factors, another mouth to feed in a household that was barely subsistent. If out of wedlock, the fathers would have been faced with subsistence payments and many ran away to join the army or to work in another parish, under an assumed name.

Also, it was not uncommon around that time that parents were in the habit of applying corporal punishment to their children, often for the smallest misdemeanour. Violence was a major element in everyday life but watching such cruelty was too much for many of the residents of Long Riston near Beverley, on the high road from Hull to Bridlington, to bear in 1799. They gathered in a pub and made a combined statement to a magistrate and the local press about the goings on at the home of the Hostler family, risking potential reprisal but feeling the need to take matters into their own hands to gain justice for a young life. Their selfless act was known legally as 'recognisance' – a bond, acknowledged in front of a justice or similar officer, the aim being to, 'Secure an action by the person named on the document.' In other words, a concerned group committed to play a part in a prosecution. At the midsummer assizes, the true nature of the cruel death of little Thomas was recorded for posterity in the careful and ornate longhand of B. Ford.

The boy's father, William, together with his wife, Jane, and his sister-in-law, Elisabeth Beal, had been regularly maltreating Thomas at their farm. Neighbours could take it no more, they had witnessed extreme cruelty over a long period and finally, they acted. Four people of the village Christopher Hall, Elisabeth Chadwell, Sarah Wray and Mary Ford stated upon oath that the three defendants had physically abused the little boy, most intensively over a period of several weeks in June of that year. That document meant that each of the accusers was bound to pay 30 pounds to his majesty George III if the action failed but that seemed unlikely as what had been done to the toddler was savage beyond belief. What the evil trio was accused of was expressed in the assize records: '… with their hands and feet and with whips and staves and sticks they did strike and kick, beat and whip over the head and neck and shoulders, back, belly, sides and posteriors, feet and other parts of the naked body of him the said Thomas Hostler in a cruel and inhuman manner giving him by such strikes, beatings and whippings, large and grievous wounds swellings and bruises on the right side of his head about the temples and several large stripes on his neck.'

These assaults, repeatedly administered over the weeks in question and most likely before wider notice, were vicious but also systematically done to affect every part of the child's body. The records make a special mention of the two women involved. 'Jane his wife and Beal did other wrongs to the said Thomas Hostler then and there, did to the great damage of Thomas Hostler and against the peace of the said Lord... did beat, wound and ill-treat so that of his life it was greatly despaired...' Between 2nd February and 10th April, it further notes that the mother savagely battered the child so that he was near death. The accounts and language used suggest there was a sadistic pleasure involved.

The boy does appear to have been dead at the time that the jury came to a decision on the cruelty but we know from a separate second action against the trio that it was the consequence. Oddly, however, the initial document hints at another mystery because initially the word 'guilty' was written after the names of all three, but was lined through after William Hostler's name with 'Not Guilty' substituted. In a second recognisance, dated 1st June, one John Dawson of Beverley swore that he would appear before the next general sessions, 'To proffer a bill of indictment against William Hostler, wife and Beal.' On that document the sentence is added: 'For the murder of the infant Thomas.'

The two women were to be pilloried in the stocks, sent to York Castle and from there transported. The pillory was often combined with whippings, as illustrations from the period make clear, and not until an act of 1837 was it abolished. With a terrible local crime such as this, repugnant to all the family values on which the community was based, there was a call for public humiliation. It would have seemed a proper administering of natural justice to the locals, that the cruel mother who had applied a whip to her child would now feel the sting of the lash on her back. Jane and Elisabeth were to spend some time in the dark hovels within York Castle and then be shunted onto a cart, taken to a ship and given the tough experience of a journey to Van Diemen's Land. Statistics at that time would have been against their survival.

As an aside to this case, it is interesting to note that in 1867, one of the most repugnant crimes in Yorkshire in this category also happened at Beverley, when Mary Haldenby thrashed her weak and half-starved son simply for stealing some morsels of food from a neighbour. Again, it was a neighbour, Mary Allen, who had contacted the local constable and she almost certainly saved the life of young William; the boy regularly beaten by his mother and her common law husband in the house.

Conversely, from all my investigations, I have chosen one women as a hero. She was a wonderful character, fired with a passion to put an end to hanging in this country. Violet van der Elst had married a rich man and lived in the magnificent Harlaxton Manor in the Vale of Belvoir. She was destined to become known to most of the police forces of England and to every prison Governor at jails in which necks were stretched. Invariably, if a hanging was imminent, there would be Mrs van der Elst, in her massive Bentley and with her chauffer, blocking a thoroughfare and calling out for reform. On one notable occasion, she campaigned for a Yorkshireman, and it was a triumph.

On 26th November, 1936, William Edwards took the life of the woman he loved. Minutes before her death, she had been weeping for fear of losing him, so much did she love him too. Why Violet van der Elst found this story such a tragic case was that the young man had no idea what he had done because he was an epileptic. Edwards was 26-years-old at the time, a man who had been drifting from job to job since leaving school. He had worked at Tankards Mill in Laisterdyke, Turners, the metal polishers, and as a labourer for Sanda Metal Co. Most recently, he had been working as a baker's assistant at Newboulds Ltd. For around six months he had kept the company of Myrtle Parker, they had been walking out regularly and he was often at her parents' house in Bierley.

Myrtle was just 20 and worked as a wool spinner. They had met at the Picturedrome in Wakefield Road and she had already agreed to his proposal of marriage even though she was legally a minor until her next birthday. Because of that, he would have to obtain a form of consent from the Marriage Registry Office. He had talked about it with Myrtle's mother and she suggested that they wait a while. Matters seem to have been good between them; there was no evidence of any acrimony.

On the fatal night the couple met at seven and, after spending some time at her home, they went out and stopped at Merrydale Road. It was there that, as they talked about their future, Myrtle began to weep and as he later said: 'Begged me to stay with her.' This upset Edwards and tipped him over into an epileptic fit. He took out his pen-knife and opened it. The report from the trial has this summary of what happened next. 'His depression deepened and, as now appears from the reconstruction, he took up the knife and whirled his arm, not knowing where the blow fell. His memory failed him. He has no recollection of what else happened.' Edwards then wandered the streets until the early morning, arriving at a friend's house and there he slept. On waking, he said to his friend: 'I have done my woman in.'

Throughout the nineteenth century there was a

continuing debate about what elements of mental illness constituted a defence of insanity and diminished responsibility. In a formative Lincolnshire case in the 1870s, a psychologist called Maudsley gave evidence and a man who had killed a village constable had his death sentence commuted as his epilepsy was shown to be the cause of his murderous actions. In Edward's case, he was sentenced to death, in spite of evidence from all different sources. First his friend, Mr Marshall, who had seen him arrive early that morning in a pitiable condition and then two medical men called as defence witnesses, insisted that Edwards' case fulfilled the criteria of epilepsy; frequent headaches, moodiness and groundless loss of temper, together with a history of many such attacks.

In court, the jury heard that four years earlier Edwards had wounded another young lady he was courting. He had stabbed her in the arm with his knife and for that he was given six month's hard labour. At that previous trial, epilepsy had been argued but had been overruled. Other witnesses had spoken including a Mr Ogden, who said that Edwards had lived with him for a few years and that: 'He used to sit in the house with his head in his hands. If asked to move, he would become bad-tempered, get up and bang things about for no reason at all... If asked what was the matter, he would make no reply.'

The police surgeon, Dr. Rimmer, said that his reading of the homicidal incident was that the man had suffered an epileptic fit. Another witness gave a clear account of a seizure. 'About a year ago I was out with Edwards in a public house. He was quite sober. Suddenly, and without reason, he threw a mug of beer at a man who had just walked past him. I hit Edwards on the side of the jaw. It was not a severe blow, but he turned pale and fell to the ground unconscious. He threw his legs and arms about and it was obvious he was in a fit. Two or three days later I spoke to him about it and he had no recollection of the incident.' Such evidence produced the kind that Edwards' counsel must have been looking for. However, it was all to no avail.

Even Myrtle's father, working at the North Bierley labour Club, saw Edwards in a fit and helped to carry him out. He and another man left him in the rain, thinking that would revive him. But the strongest statement came from Edwards' mother, Amy, who said that he had had two fits when he was just four years old and that he was three years old before he could talk. She said that as he grew older he would have frightening mood-swings and that he tended to fly into a rage if he was disturbed. He had left home in 1934 and lived with his sister, Mrs Ogden in Lilac Grove Street.

But the most considerable medical statement came from Dr. Frederick Eurich of Edinburgh University and consulting physician at Bradford Royal Infirmary. He said at the trial: 'I have spent three and a half years in a large asylum controlling 2,000 patients, made a special study of mental diseases in England and in Germany… From the facts put before me, I have arrived at the following conclusion, namely that it is highly probable that Edwards suffers from occasional attacks of epilepsy…' Eurich explained that people like Edwards suffer from loss of memory and waves of depression. He also added that in these states, the depression was likely to lead to periodic fits of violence. Apparently, Edwards lifted Myrtle over a wall after the attack but recalled nothing of that the next day. There had been complete normality earlier on the day of the homicide. Edwards had been at the home of Myrtle's sister, Gladys, and they had both walked to a draper's shop in Tong Street, where Edwards paid for some gloves he had ordered.

Edwards' last statement in court was that for as long as he could remember, he had never felt, 'normal in health.' He also stressed that he drank very little alcohol, so that was never a factor in the violence. He was condemned to death but that was later overturned by the Home Secretary. The campaigner for the abolition of capital punishment, Mrs van der Elst, wrote in her account of the case, 'I hope Edwards will be given plenty of work to do to keep his mind occupied, so that he can work out his own salvation.' Not all killers in the throes of epilepsy were so fortunate. In 1934, also in Bradford, Louis Hamilton killed his wife at Stott Hill and claimed an attack of petit mal, the less severe form of epilepsy, was the reason. That did not save him from the gallows and he met an appointment with executioner Thomas Pierrepoint in Armley.

Then there are the incidences of poisoning and one in particular, that of 'The Yorkshire Witch' which is one of the few large-scale Leeds crime stories. York Castle has a long and often grim, disturbing history, a formidable and dark place that tells a great deal about a turbulent period in English social history. One of the most evil residents of that dungeon was the Leeds poisoner, Mary Bateman, said by many to be a witch. She was born Mary Harker in 1768 and one writer noted, 'From an early age she developed great quickness which, instead of taking a direct course and developing into intelligence, was warped into low cunning.' Violence was rife at this time, with highwaymen and footpads everywhere and riots always likely to break out among the underclass. Bateman's was one of the most heinous cases of a young mother who murdered to make her way in life and dabbled in black magic. At five o'clock on a chill Monday morning in March, 1809, 41-year-old Mary Bateman was brought from her cell in York to keep her date with the hangman. Knowing that pregnant women were spared the noose, she had tried to 'plead her belly' to save her neck, but it was no use. A massive crowd gathered, they wanted their entertainment and to see justice done.

The jury were in no doubt that the woman originally from Aisenby, near Thirsk had poisoned Rebecca Perigo of Bramley, Leeds. Her crime had been carried out in such a protracted and cunningly planned way that her evil was deemed the more outrageous and callous. Mary had schemed to defraud Perigo, and was clearly aiming to poison another victim who was suspecting her of the crime, when she was apprehended. When arrested, a phial of deadly poison was found on her. Her offences were seen as even more devious and damnable when it was learned that she had attempted to practise witchcraft while she was in prison. She had extorted money from a young girl who wanted to see her sweetheart by sewing a charm and coins into her dress, something that would mysteriously force the young man she loved to come and visit her in the gaol. Naturally, when it didn't work, the material was torn open and the coins were gone, into Mary's pocket. She had the knack of being able to put on a performance when required, and also to be as nimble and deceptive as the most skilled pickpocket.

Mary, while living in Leeds, did very well for herself by conning all kinds of people. One Victorian account of her crimes describes a typical ruse. 'The subject of this narrative contrived to ingratiate herself, as she well knew how, into the good graces of a family of the name of Kitchin, two maiden ladies of the Quaker persuasion who kept a small linen shop near St Peter's Square in Leeds. There is every reason to suppose that she had deluded these unfortunate young women with some idea of her skill in looking into futurity... For some time Mary was the confidante of the Misses

Kitchin… In the early part of September, 1803 one of the young women became very ill; Mary Bateman procured for her medicines…These medicines were of a powerful efficacy and in the course of less than one week, Miss Kitchin died…'

Mary and her husband had lived in High Court Lane when they first came to Leeds and from there she started her life of crime, first stealing from a lodger and then working to obtain property by deception. She even took money under false pretences from a poor widow and callously saw the children of her victim sent to the workhouse. At the trial, when Mary claimed she was pregnant, the scene devolved from solemnity into farce. The judge wanted a group of matrons in the court to examine Mary to prove her condition and, as no-one wanted to be involved, they began to shuffle out of the courtroom with some indignation. But the law prevailed. The judge ordered the doors to be shut so that the women had no choice but to comply and Mary was duly inspected, pronounced not with child, and the sentence passed. The trial had lasted for 11 hours before the judge donned his black cap.

The gaoler, who was with her on her last night, noted that she wrote a letter to her husband and sent her wedding ring home to be given to her daughter. She had her youngest child in the cell with her, to suckle, and it was a scene that the ordinary (the officer who interviewed and monitored statements by prisoners) noted with feelings of sympathy. However, he also remarked on her silences regarding the crimes she had committed, and felt sure that she knew much more about other suspicious deaths connected with her activities. In the end, those secrets went to the grave with her.

At that time, noted killers and footpads – a robber or thief specialising in pedestrian victims – attracted great crowds at their death throes and Mary Bateman was no exception. Though there were no friends to swing on her legs and quicken her death, there was, nevertheless, a significant attendance to prove her status as a local celebrity. A big crowd had travelled from Leeds to see justice done. The hanging took place at the new drop, behind the castle. It was eerily quiet when Mary said a prayer but a shudder went through the crowd when she begged for mercy and shouted out that she was innocent.

Her body was taken back to Leeds by hearse to be used for medical dissection but with such celebrity, death provoked a general curiosity to view the body and Mary's was a particularly successful crowd-puller. So many people came to look at her corpse that the money raised was £80. 14s, then a great amount. It was given to the General Infirmary. Mary Bateman was destined to be the subject of ballads, chapbooks and tales by the fireside for many years to come throughout Yorkshire, at a time when killers and robbers attracted more attention and sensation than conventional heroes. She became the stuff of myth and tall tales and it appeared that she was full of tricks and cons, even on one occasion having a hen appear to lay an egg with 'Christ is Coming' written on the shell. She possessed another quality of the worst killer, stealth and subtlety, winning allegiance and trust before she struck with her deadly poison.

The fact that Mary's corpse was taken to Leeds Infirmary for dissection anchors her story in brutal reality, and keeps it embedded in the social history of the time, when medics needed cadavers so desperately that the body-snatchers got to work. Names such as Burke and Hare, also found their place in folk tales. The need also created other associated talents like that of Herbert Davies, the inventor who came up with a device to fasten the dead into their coffins so that Burke and Hare would have a tough job wrenching them out, all leading to moral panics about the

'Resurrection Men' in the 1830s, especially as cholera was endemic at that time.

Another to embed themselves equally as prominently in the public consciousness was Jack the Ripper. So much so that his Yorkshire counterpart, Peter Sutcliffe, carried that same feared moniker almost 90 years later. In Patricia Cornwell's book on the Ripper, she argued that Jack came north with Henry Irving's theatre company and was in Bradford when the murder of a young boy occurred. It was a most brutal killing and with all the trappings and hallmarks of Jack despite being a long way from his usual patch.

Very early in the morning, just after Christmas 1888, eight-year-old John Gill of Thorncliff Road went for a ride on a milk-cart and his mother never saw him alive again. He had been seen playing but also, menacingly, talking to a man; a stranger to the area by all accounts. The family soon felt the distress of his absence and feared the worst, placing a poster on view with a physical description of John. His body was found by Joe Buckle, a butcher, who was cleaning a stable when he spied a bundle and, looking closer, realised that it was a corpse. Most noticeable on first inspection was that one ear had been cut off. He ran for help. Examined by officers at the scene, it was found that there had been extreme mutilation of the boy; his stomach had been cut open and vital organs placed on him. He had been repeatedly cut, stabbed in the chest, and there was a rough noose around his neck.

This is where the complex business of the massive number of Ripper accounts written about his modus operandi figure in the story. The pathology certainly makes the Gill murder a contender for being classified as a Ripper killing. Dr. Bond, writing about Mary Kelly's body, for example, noted that, 'The viscera were found in various parts... the liver between the feet and the spleen by the left side of the body.' By the time of the Gill case, police were walking in Whitechapel in pairs; five killings had taken place, the last in November, just a month before the Bradford death.

At the end of November, one of the Ripper letters had in it, 'I shall do another murder on some young youth such as printing lads who work in the city. I did write you once before… I shall do them worse than the women, I shall take their hearts…' But the problem with Cornwell's use of the Ripper letters in associating the Bradford case with Jack is that she talks of them as if it is certain that there was one author. Perhaps that is why she dismisses the most tantalising scrap of detail in poor John Gill's murder, that a piece of a Liverpool newspaper was used to wrap part of the body. Even more fascinating, the paper had a name on it: W. Mason, Derby Road.

Those Ripperologists who think that the man behind the moniker was James Maybrick, merchant of Liverpool, would see an obvious link. Recent writing on Maybrick, and notably the new work done by experts on 'The Ripper Diary' would seem to confirm that there is no factual reference to a Bradford connection. The Ripper letters in the hand that Cornwell believes was that of the painter Walter Sickert also contains one text which reads, 'I riped [sic] up a little boy in Bradford' and another one has the date, January 16, Bradford.' What we most likely have here is that well-known phenomenon in homicide, the copycat crime. As far as the Bradford connection is concerned, the events could have turned out tragically for the prime suspect in the city Bill Barrett, the dairyman, but he was cleared as the only evidence was circumstantial. Even if the killing was a copycat murder, then the identity of the real killer remains a mystery, and the Gill case is still in the annals of unsolved crimes.

Related to it is the case of Maria Coroner from October,

1888. Hers shows the way in which a total mesmeric relationship to a serial killer's image and foul deeds will attract a certain type of perverted 'fan' with a bent towards obsession. She too was from Bradford and was found to be the author of a letter purporting to be from Jack the Ripper. She also collected dark souvenirs of criminal cases. Her fate was a conviction and a £20 fine, which would have a value today of £900.

The Ripper did attract sinister copycat psychopaths. One case concerns a deranged man called Fred Brett who, in November, 1888, was possessed by a rage to do some mischief. He worked as a railway labourer in Halifax and, on one occasion, took hold of a knife and began throwing it around. When he then felt that his wife was being a little too close to some fellow workers, he killed her. Asked if he had anything to say, he replied: 'Yes, I have done it and it can't be undone. I was only playing at Jack the Ripper!' He was subsequently hanged by James Billington inside Armley gaol.

More recently, Bruce Robinson, creator of the cult film, *Withnail and I*, has delved deeply into the identity of Jack the Ripper. His conclusion is that the mystery man was Michael Maybrick, songwriter and well-known member of the masonic lodge, very much familiar with the theatrical world, and who was in the provinces at certain crucial times. More than coincidental for the Gill murder.

Peter Sutcliffe's years of slaughter created understandable widespread panic and such a proliferation of spin-off stories that almost anyone with a Geordie accent or who was a travelling salesman staying in a lonely bed and breakfast became suspect. I was teaching in a college of further education at the time but there were freakish and disturbing links between the course of my life in those killing years and the scenes of crime Sutcliffe chose. I had done teacher training in Huddersfield and was often walking past the station wood yard where one such attack took place. I courted my wife in Savile Park, Halifax, staying in a terrace house just a hundred yards from the Park where the killer took the life of a teenager. I lived for a year in Headingley, five minutes' walk from where Sutcliffe changed the nature of his victims and killed a student, and had played football in the Leeds Sunday League, often turning out at Soldier's Field, Roundhay — another murder scene.

Foolishly, during the height of Sutcliffe's regime of terror, I mentioned all this to my class of young women trainee nurses at the college. They became suspicious and whispered in my presence for weeks afterwards. Even more eerie was the fact that on the night of the Halifax murder, my sister-in-law had offered to go out and fetch some fish and chips for supper which would have entailed a walk across Savile Park just as young Josephine Whitaker was killed there.

Later, when researching the Yorkshire Ripper for my book, *Britain's Most Notorious Prisoners*, I learned just how close to my roots the monster's story had stretched. In a family photograph album there is a picture of Churwell Working Men's Club football team, dated around 1950. My father is in the picture and the sister of one of his team-mates was subsequently related to a Ripper victim. I recall seeing him play on the Tanhouse pitch just between Churwell and the Elland Road football ground and the post-war prefabs by the cemetery at Gelderd Road. This is only a footnote to the Ripper story but it permanently touched me and mine, as similar connections did to so many Yorkshire people. It is impossible to evade the repugnant essence of depravity that still hangs over local memories. It is almost as if the Leeds and Bradford streets, and their counterparts in Huddersfield and Halifax, retain some traces of his evil, in the way ghosts linger in oppressed houses.

This is not the only connection of Ripper stories to Yorkshire. A Jack the Ripper suspect is linked with Hull. In 1891, the press were convinced that Frederick Deeming was the cloaked killer. He had been in Hull prison before going to Melbourne, where he was arrested and charged with murder. Deeming had slaughtered first of all in Rainhill, Liverpool and then again across the world. In 1890, under the name of Harry Lawson, he was in prison in Hull and the governor, Mr Webster, went out to Melbourne to help the police in identification. The press there reported, 'At this visible accusation, Deeming was notably disconcerted.' Some journalists blamed Hull for unleashing the beast Deeming on Australia after letting him out but he had served his term and there was no knowledge of any murder in Liverpool at that time. Deeming had been sentenced to nine months for obtaining a diamond by fraud from Reynoldson's jewellers in Hull. At the time of his arrest, the local press asserted that he, 'Had been extradited from Montevideo, whither he had absconded...'

After the killing of Emily Mather in Melbourne, there was an effort by the Australian police to communicate with their counterparts in Lancashire where Deeming had murdered his wife and children. Deeming had a habit of burying his victims under the floorboards. He was hanged in Victoria's capital and there is still quite a lobby among Ripperologists to keep Deeming up there as a main suspect for Jack. Hull historian Mike Covell has been busy looking at this and other links of Ripper references to the city, including a letter written to the police stating that the Ripper was coming to Hull to kill again, but he is not one of the most favoured suspects. In 2014, Russell Edwards in his book, *Naming Jack the Ripper*, notes that Deeming was, 'An evil man with no redeeming features: he was a conman, a thief, a braggard, a bigamist. It all sounded to me at the time, as if he could be a suitable candidate.' Then Edwards adds, 'But after six years of trawling through books and records, I was unable to find anything to take the Ripper connection forward.'

It is not difficult to find footnotes to the Ripper stories which lead one to see a new suspect. When researching for my book on Conan Doyle, I looked at the lives and interests of the men who were members of the Crimes Club, among whom was the author of Sherlock Holmes and several criminologists as well as writers. One of the members was George R. Sims, prolific producer of plays and novels, and known to the general public as the humorist Dagonet in the popular press. Today he is remembered as the author of 'It was Christmas Day in the Workhouse.' Sims, in his autobiography, writes about buying a coffee from a stall-holder who he knew and remembering the man saying that there had been a Ripper murder that night and joking that George looked exactly like the picture circulated by the police and press. So the fascination grows.

I started learning to write crime stories around 15 years after those latest Ripper tales and one aspect that has stayed with me is the significance of a crime scene, not necessarily forensically but as a backdrop.

Even a minute's contemplation of a demarcated space where someone has died by violence has a peculiar resonance. Sometimes it feels as if there is a music there, for me the chamber music of Robert Schumann, a man whose mind was awry. He went from being *distrait* to openly, agonizingly, mentally ill, and tried to drown himself in the river Rhine in 1854, to be taken from there to an asylum. At other crime scenes contemplation creates some kind of ethereal, spiritual feeling. Detectives will say that a murder scene speaks to them, that they need to observe rather than just look at what is before them.

The writer is essentially a storyteller and for that to emerge, what starts to matter is the route to the murder scene – in every sense; the landscape, as it were, of a person whose destiny is to be a victim. Leeds has had its own examples and one in particular stands out. It was first fully recorded by Andy Owens, and then I described the events in my book, *DNA Crime Investigations*. It was the killing of Mary Gregson in 1977. She worked as a cleaner at Salt's Mill and had a mere 600 yard walk there which included the canal towpath, and there was her vulnerability. She was attacked, and strangled with a ligature and her body hurled into the water, although it wasn't until three years later that the perpetrator was caught via DNA. That piece of banking tells the researcher and the writer a great deal. The closeness of the water limits the scope for scrutiny and it also opens up plenty of imaginative reconstruction. The killer of Mary Gregson did leave a genetic clue and as the old Locard's principle states, every contact leaves a trace.

In this catalogue of memorable tales, there is one which illustrates the other than horrific – the crime which is almost farcical. In this case, it's all about dripping. There were times in the Victorian period when, in spite of the demands of the law and the innate sense of the importance of order and peace, the much distressed working class found it too much to tolerate when an injustice was seen to be done. Often disturbances were in response to the hand of the legalities being so heavy it offended decency and reason. But then there were other causes of acts of rebellion and destruction that stemmed from an incident very small.

Dripping has long had a place in the Yorkshire culinary repertoire and older Leeds people still talk fondly of their youth, when society was less health conscious, and a treat was a dripping sandwich; salty, rich and satisfying. Back in 1865 dripping had dozens of uses for the matriarch of the house feeding her usually large family. In the case of domestic servants, taking a little dripping from the cooking done for the employer was common practice and generally accepted. But not so in the household of Henry Chorley in Park Square. On this occasion, in February of that year, he refused to follow that common practice.

Eliza Stafford, was Chorley's 50-year-old cook and when she roasted a joint for him, she expected a portion of the dripping to take home. Chorley was a powerful man in the city, a magistrate and also a respected surgeon. But respect was lost on this occasion when she was sent to Armley Gaol, convicted of stealing two pounds of the stuff and given one month's imprisonment. She was quite new to his employment having been there for only a few months. When challenged about the matter she said that she was allowed it, 'As a perquisite, though I said nothing about that when I was first engaged to do the work.'

All hell broke out around Chorley's place when word spread. What made things worse was that her trial had been held in camera and the Mayor of Leeds himself had been on the bench. The spark was lit by an article which reported at the time, 'In a few days after the committal of the woman attention was called to the case, in a spirit of indignation, by one of the local papers which is best known for its publication of sensational stories and in its indulgence of caricature sketches of local personages ...' The report also noted that newsboys were shouting out scraps of gossip and jokes, and that people were chatting about the affair in disgust. In the street this rhyme was heard:

'Now all you cooks and servant girls wot's very fond of
tipping
Don't take your master's scraps of fat and boil 'em down
for dripping:
For if you do bear this in mind, the magistrates won't fail
To try you in a private court and send you off to gaol.'

Graffiti appeared on the walls of the Chorley home and on
plenty of others, stating, 'A month's imprisonment for 2lbs
of dripping.' Things escalated so that Chorley was vilified in
the street and harassed and bullied. He received threatening
letters and placards began to appear expressing the view that
Leeds people should assemble for a large celebration when
Eliza came out of prison. But even before that, pressure
mounted. A large and aggressive crowd gathered outside
Chorley's house. At first they shouted insults and then threw
missiles at it including snowballs and stones. Chorley had the
courage to come out and face them, he tried to talk to them
and explain his position on the matter but to no avail, they
threw dirt at him. When the police arrived the mob gradually
dispersed, but there was worse to come.

Late in the evening of 22nd February, a huge crowd
assembled outside Armley Gaol expecting Mrs Stafford to
appear, but she did not. The mob had planned a celebration
but instead found that their friend was still locked up, or so
they thought; in fact she had been let out earlier so as not to
cause a scene. After that the crowd were determined to go
again to Chorley's house and this time contrived to hang a
bottle and an old dripping–pan to the end of a long pole. The
police who stood by took a very long time to move the crowd
away. Still the Leeds populace were not satisfied. The next
day stones were thrown at the Chorleys' windows pushing
the authorities to take action. To make matters worse, the

Chief Constable, Mr Bell, while trying to help move the crowd, fell heavily and dislocated a shoulder. The crowd mentality took over and several were crushed and trampled. One man, under the feet of the mob, was so seriously injured he had to be taken to the infirmary. The police could not cope.

The army at York were called for by telegraph and, come the evening, men from the 8th Hussars were in Leeds having travelled by train. The authorities were not finished there with extra police from Bradford called for as well. There was a feeling that the riot had been calmed by the time local journalists posted their reports, however, late that night a crowd of about 2,000 gathered outside the town hall and shouted out insults. The police took the brunt of the anger and as they were moved away, a stone cut deeply into the temple of an officer. There were several arrests as destruction and lawlessness filled the city.

All this time, Mrs Stafford had been elsewhere. She had left Leeds much earlier, going to Scarborough where her daughter lived. The *Times* reflected that she showed good sense, 'Preferring to avoid the questionable honours the crowd intended to confer upon her.' The politic action afterwards as her whereabouts became known and reactions calmed, saw sound advice from the police and prison Governor. It was decided that the five men arrested should not be dealt with seriously. There was a feeling of regret for the mean and thoughtless use of power by a bench of influential men of high status pursuing an easy victim. The newspapers had imagined and recreated that scene in the eyes of the public and the formula was one for creating extreme disorder on the streets of Leeds. We have to remember that the rallying workers were chief protagonists but the so-called 'underclass' was another matter entirely. Usually when disorder hit the streets it was the lowest social order, desperate and pushed to the end of their tether by economic pressures such as the price of bread and the lack of job opportunities who were in the forefront of disturbances. The Leeds dripping riots, though, saw decent people goaded into militancy and rage over the harsh administering of the letter of the law and the need to exert power.

Of all such socially-motivated Yorkshire crimes encountered, one character stands out. In 1812, the clothing industry of the West Riding faced the implications of the arrival of new machinery in the finishing processes of manufacture, with many of the work force resolved to fight the changes. What some of them did in their zeal to survive was bring a reign of terror to villages and mills from the Pennines to the Halifax and Bradford areas. In order to defeat them, the forces of law had to bring in the militia, such was the fear generated across the county. It was a time of particularly strained and repressive economic measures and poorer families across the board were suffering. Oddly, many of the christened Luddites were the better off, but they feared the future and were not prepared to stand idly by while the greater macroeconomic factors of production sought to crush them.

Rarely in the criminal annals of the county has there been such a clear, raw confrontation between an underclass and their bosses; the resentment went deep. Leaders were needed to harness it and they took their name from a fabled character called Ned Ludd who reputedly led similar machine-wrecking attacks in Nottingham. In the Spen Valley, a man named Mellor emerged who was to conduct a campaign of profound fear-instilling aggression against those employers who had installed new machinery. The focus for the campaign was the trade linked to the cloth finishing processes, in particular the shearers, of whom Mellor was one. This was a skilled business, demanding the expert use of large and unwieldy shears for trimming. Mellor quickly realised that the essence of success in these attacks was secrecy, difficult as the communities along the valley were close-knit. He therefore had his men black their faces, always wear hats and attack by night. The reign of terror lasted for some time and the local magistrates were at a loss what to do. But the chain of command broadened and the reaction of the authorities spread from the West Riding to the militia, then to the Lord Lieutenant of the county at Wentworth Woodhouse, and eventually to the Home Secretary.

After various delays that gave the Luddites the upper hand, paranoia eventually led to positive action. First, a repressive group of militia conducted their own reprisals and then, with a new Home Secretary, Lord Sidmouth, taking office, the establishment began to create an equal measure of fear in their opponents. It became a case of the magistrates finding men willing to give information and Sidmouth was keen on the use of spies functioning as agents provocateurs. Matters were made worse as deaths occurred, notably the murder of a factory-owner called Horsfall. Mellor, along with William Thorpe and Thomas Smith, was charged. Horsfall had been attacked on the road and shot by men in the undergrowth. Witnesses came forward to implicate Mellor, not least a particular turncoat and petty thief from the village of Flockton. The trio were found guilty. One contemporary commentator wrote, 'It is impossible to read the details of this and the other Luddite cases without shuddering at the cold-hearted and systematic manner in which the murders were debated and agreed on.' Mellor, Smith and Thorpe were hanged on 8th January, 1813. They were led to the scaffold still in their irons and all went down on their knees after the chaplain asked them to pray. Mellor said: 'Some of my enemies may be here. If they be, I freely forgive them, and all the world, and I hope the world will forgive me.' The bodies were taken to York County Hospital for dissection.

On 16th January, 14 men were hanged on the conviction of taking an illegal oath and the destruction of a mill. In addition, there was a charge of riot. Eight men were found guilty of riot and destruction at Cartwright's Mill, the story featuring in Charlotte Bronte's novel, Shirley. There were attempts to provide alibis when several defence witnesses were called but all that failed and it took the jury just five minutes to decide on a guilty verdict. As was noted by several historians in earlier times, all the men were married and left young children fatherless. The word Luddite entered the language such was the impact of that year of terror when the middle classes in the valleys of the West Riding could not sleep easily in their beds.

The man responsible for the hangings was William Curry, who was in that post for over 30 years. He was known to the rabble as 'Mutton' Curry, and he too had his problems. In 1821 he was set to hang a robber, Bill Brown, and the local *Gazette* reported that Curry had partaken rather too much to drink. '... in proceeding from the County execution which he had conducted with his usual propriety, to the place of execution for the City, he was recognised by the populace, who were posting with unsatiated appetites from one feast of death to another... they hustled and insulted the executioner to such a degree... that he arrived nearly exhausted, and with nerves quite inadequate to the task he had to perform... Under these circumstances it was that he unfortunately applied the stimulus of spirits... His head became affected and he exhibited a spectacle much to be regretted.' He was unsteady as he stood on the scaffold, fixing the rope, and he called to the crowd: 'Some of you come up and I'll try it!'

5

•

A MOST INFAMOUS
MURDERESS

Strangeways, Manchester, June, 1926. Let's slip into the mind
of a woman about to die, revealed by her final jottings.

'She had been told, by some of her customers, about
hangings. Her line of work tended to attract criminals and
bad 'uns of all kinds, as well as the gents, though they all had
the stink of sweat on their shirts. Yes, she had listened to
descriptions of the gallows and the hangmen. One man, a
justice's clerk he was from Wakefield, he used to tell tales
while he was fucking her. As the old bed squeaked and
crackled, he used to go on about mucky women and how he
loved 'em. I like a bit o' dirt about 'em, Louie... like you, filthy
bloody knees. First time I saw you I noticed your knees have
not been washed for years... Men – bloody pigs they were.
Led by their cocks, talked shit, weened on lies since being
babbies.'

She had never been one for words and writing. School had been just tolerable and there she had learned to have a 'nice clear hand' with the cursive, looped and crossed words flowing neatly between the lines across the paper. Borstal had meant some schooling again. Some good folk had tried to show her that neat handwriting and good manners helped in being somebody in the world. She had taken no notice of words then.

But a year ago, before she sat in her cell in Strangeways prison, Louie had taken notice of poems and fine words. Mr Byrne, the bookseller, had let her have some printed sheets from his drawers – one a poem about the *RMS Lusitania* that was sunk by the Germans. Yes, she had liked the poems Mr Bryne used to quote. He was like a schoolteacher, full of clever talk. He was nothing like other men, Mr Byrne. She had often wondered about what kept them going, these clever types. He talked like he'd been to a good school. When she had called in for tea and a natter, along with Lily when they were both scatty and a bit free and easy with their favours, all he had wanted was to read aloud a few stirring poems. She had giggled like a schoolgirl and he'd loved that. Why couldn't she have had a dad like Mr Byrne? It was all a lottery this life.

It had all been so easy, at first, earning brass from quick fumbles up back-streets, yanking off desperate blokes too pissed to have more than a limp sausage. Most of all, it had all been a laugh. Now, with maybe just a few weeks left on this earth, she asked for a little notebook, and when the wardress asked what did she want it for, Louie had said: 'To write my life story.' She had heard the wardress say to another prisoner: 'What does she want to do that for... who wants to read about a murderess?' But Louie didn't let that talk upset her. No, she set about writing all the things that would explain why she had done the things she had and what had happened that night at the end of March when Lily had been killed. She soon prompted her memory into working, beginning with her husband. The only problem was the marks - the dots and that, she thought. She wasn't sure about where they went. But the words came easily: 'My husband went back this time to India and died the Friday as my son was born... now as my boy was three months old I was sent to prison again for six months...'

'Hey, Calvert...' It was the woman from the cell on the end of the landing. She was a nasty piece of work. 'Hey Calvert... you know the night before they stretch your neck... well, they give you a glass of wine instead of milk.... nice eh?' Then she made that queer noise in her throat, as if she was being throttled – just what she deserved.

Then there it was, the notebook. It was like a child would have at school, dull card covers and then bold, blue-lined pages. Just looking at it brought back the memories of the attempts to write lines, putting the slopes and curls of the letters between them. Yes, once she had written out, hundreds of times, 'Tears, idle tears, I know not what they mean.' She promised herself that if she ever got the chance, she would track down that Lord Tennyson and tell him off. 'Just put an 'X'... there's no words in thee!' The wardress again, enjoying her cheek. Louie ignored her and looked at her first finished page. She thought, 'This will be my book for them all to read when I'm not here, all the nosy Parkers what was at the trial and all the bloody neighbours back in Leeds.' She was saying what she wanted to say before that jury, but never had a chance.

Louie Calvert's tale has been told many times but it's always the same one, full of idle thinking. The untruths have been repeated, made into myths. In true crime stories, it's such a simple affair to take the events as they have always been and add some flourishes. But what about getting close? Close enough to smell the muck in the gutters and the fog on the old brick around the Leeds streets as the world went into the 1920s, riding the strikes and the sadness, the aching loss of the war effects lingering on, and the sense that nothing is really worthwhile except having a good time. But still, you need to know what story has been told – how Louie has been explained.

The outline contains all the accepted thinking. I'm telling it again so that I can then challenge it, as a detective would re-opening a cold case. Lily Waterhouse was 40 years old in 1923 when Louie Calvert knocked on her door. Lily's husband had died a year before and she had lived in Amberley Road in Leeds, for 14 years. She had no idea that Calvert had come to stay with her as part of a ruse to fool Louie's husband, Arty, into thinking that she was with her sister in Dewsbury and that she was having a baby. Louie Calvert was indulging in one of her complex deceptions, she was not only leading a life of deep ambiguity but she was someone who enjoyed lying so that she could feel the thrills of escape from the mundanity of real life.

Louie had been a housekeeper for a Mr Frobisher the year before and he was found dead in the River Aire in July, 1922. With hindsight it seems peculiar that the coroner did not ask more questions about the corpse. There was a wound on the back of his head and he had no boots on. At the inquest, little Louie appeared and stated that she had pawned the boots for a few shillings. All this was very strange because Frobisher lived a mile or so away from where his body was found. Had he walked bare-foot to his death? Was it suicide? It is astounding that the verdict at the inquest was death by misadventure.

That had been the first appearance of Louie Calvert in the records and she was destined to become far more prominent than that. She moved on from Frobisher's place to marry Arty Calvert in Hunslet and now there she was, away from home, pretending to be pregnant. She had two children already, one living with her and Arty, Kenneth; and a girl, Annie, who resided in Dewsbury. So here then was a strange situation, a woman of 33 turning up, wanting a room, and then, unknown to the landlady, her guest was trying to work out how to possess a baby that she could pass off as her own. The obvious thing to do was to advertise, as you would for any goods and the lineage in the Leeds paper did indeed work. A teenager from Pontefract had given birth to a little girl in Leeds and her mother saw Louie's advert. It did not take long to arrange for an adoption; all Louie had to do was lie low in her lodgings and wait until the baby was with her. In this phase of her life we see Louie Calvert the odd performer, acting a role. The situation was extremely bizarre, a married woman living under an assumed identity in another part of the city in which her husband and real home were, pretending to be there in order to care for her new-born, that was currently in hospital to someone else. Yet, strangely, that would have seemed a plausible tale at the time. Many young babies were ill with all kinds of maladies, from diphtheria to scarlet fever, kept in hospital in intensive care whilst the mother would visit.

Louie's love of performance, of escaping from herself and going into a role, was changing. Formerly, when she worked for Frobisher, she wore Salvation Army clothes and acted the part well. She was also a compulsive thief and her pawning of Frobisher's boots had been just one of many visits to the pawnbroker's with stolen items. Another startling aspect of Louie Calvert is that, though she was very short and thin, just five feet tall, her personality was forceful and assertive. She was capable of instilling fear in people. So much was this evident to Lily Waterhouse that she was at first frightened to say anything when she began to notice that various objects had disappeared from her home. But Lily gathered some determination when she found pawn tickets clearly relating to her missing objects. This was a time when many working people were in dire straits and habits such as pawning a best Sunday suit almost on a weekly basis was one desperate way of keeping a little ready cash in the house. Louie was reported to the police but ultimately returned to her lodgings, packed up her bags and her baby, and went home to her house in Railway Place, Hunslet. It was what happened in the interim that made the headline writers sharpen their pencils.

As earlier investigators into the heinous crime that followed have speculated, how on earth she managed to be so prominent and sociable around Leeds in the time she was supposed to be having a child in Dewsbury is amazing; she was a familiar sight to many, and distinctive in her build and her speech.

Before Louie Calvert was to leave to go back to her husband, she had some business to attend to in Amberley Road, and it was a deadly affair.

It was just before Easter when Louie left the Waterhouse home. Lily had been seen going into her house on the Wednesday night ahead of Good Friday. In those terraces neighbours saw and heard a great deal, there was very little privacy and people were sensitive to any unusual sounds; domestic arguments were hard to keep private. On this occasion, a neighbour heard noises in the lodger's room and then saw Louie as she left the house, carrying her new baby. Louie told the neighbour that Lily was upset but that she was going home. She explained the odd noises by lying, saying that she and Lily had been moving a bed.

At last Arty Calvert had his wife back and also what he thought was his baby, little Dorothy. But the next morning Arty saw that there was some luggage in the house that had not been there the night before. Unbelievably, Louie Calvert had returned to Amberley Road in the early hours and collected a large suitcase. At this stage in her deceptions, Louie was clumsy. She was seen by several people, despite the early time of day, and they would be valuable statements later on in the tale. Even more surprising as we re-read the case today, she left a note. If she had not done so, then the chances are that the dual life she had constructed may well have kept her out of suspicion when the police started looking for the little woman who had lodged in Amberley Road.

They started looking for her very soon after her dawn reappearance at the lodgings, as Lily Waterhouse had not appeared for the summons she'd issued against Louie. The police came to check out why and discovered the woman's corpse, lying on the floor in a bedroom with blood everywhere, including up the walls. It was clear she had been battered on the head. The hallmark was there at the scene, though it was not perceived at the time: Lily Waterhouse was fully dressed – apart from her boots. There had clearly been a violent struggle and the landlady had fought with some tenacity as she was badly bruised, and it had taken several heavy blows to finish her. It is somewhat difficult to accept, bearing in mind the physical stature of Louie that she could have been a sole culprit, if one at all; Lily Waterhouse had also been strangled. The killer, the police noticed, had cut up cloth to use to tie her hands and feet, yet there must have been something else used to strangle the woman as the ligature marks on her neck were wider than that caused by a strip of cloth. It is a gruesome thought that the noises heard by the neighbours were almost certainly the movements of the dying woman's limbs as she was shaking in her death-throes. The sounds of feet thrashing on wooden boards would surely have meant that the attack would have been heard through paper-thin walls.

What previously had been accepted as the image of a widow leading a lonely and rather impoverished life, turned out to be something very different as questions were asked during the ensuing investigation. In fact, some of Lily's previous lodgers had been ladies of the night. These were tough times in Leeds and there was high unemployment. A widow with a low income would no doubt have been tempted to take in guests who would pay well and no questions would be asked. But Lily was also unusual in that she had not been the isolated figure one might suppose. Since her husband's death, she too had received lots of visitors, some dabbling in spiritualism. Neighbours, answering questions about her character seemed eager to mention the shadier side of Lily's life, even to the point of one commenting that: 'She was not a clean woman.' Understandably, those comments and implications led to the police to look for suspects among the clientele she had mixed with in the recent past.

Neighbours also began to recall the lodger with the baby and there was the matter of the letter Louie had left. She was soon tracked down and this woman who had been enjoying the strange thrills of moving from one name and identity to another for some time, escaping the reality she perhaps feared, opened her door one night in April 1925 to find D.I. Pass standing there. Louie was an unprepossessing sight and, as investigations into her background continued, there was a terrible irony in the fact that one of her assumed names had been Edith Thompson, the celebrated, sophisticated, articulate and murderous accomplice who had been hanged at Holloway in 1923. In contrast, little Louie Calvert was ill-looking, underweight and coarse and, amazingly, was wearing Mrs Waterhouse's boots when she answered the door. The beginning of the end of her criminal career was at hand.

The police work was extremely efficient, initially working on the adoption and the Dewsbury connection and Louie was arrested. At the Town Hall, disbelieving Arty learned all the real facts for the first time, and while he was absorbing all that and wondering how he would tell young Kenneth, Louie was insisting, when charged with murder, that she didn't do it. The trial at Leeds was in front of Mr Justice Wright. The court learned that for the two years before she moved in with Calvert, Louie had lived hand-to-mouth but had realised that there were ways of exploiting poverty and existing in various roles and guises. Possibly one of the most interesting and informative of these was her time as a Salvation Army woman. Rather than a deep religious conviction, she sought for them to look after her and the organisation was easy for her to exploit. She went to Alpha Street Hall meetings but it was all a front. Often small details speak volumes and in this case, it has to be noted that she had even stolen her bonnet from a proper Salvation Army member. The author of the most exhaustive account of this case has mentioned a neighbour who knew Louie well and she testified that, despite her stature, Louie had violent tempers and was capable of changing her mood rapidly, and of using bad language. The witness said that the obscenities from her were so extreme that she had banned Louie from coming into her home.

When Louie Calvert was asked if she had anything to say before the sentence was passed, she said simply: 'Yes, Sir, I'm pregnant.' It indicates the naïve facility she had for a child-like defence when cornered. Saying an infantile thing like that was tantamount to admitting that her sense of reality was very slender and her inner fantasy, feeding the outer criminal who was a predator on the streets of Leeds, was a truly frightening aspect of her personality. She had constantly avoided any statements in the witness box with the argument that she was ill – and now supposedly pregnant. A medical inspection was deemed essential and Dr Hoyland Smith went to examine her in the court cell with a woman also attending. She was from a jury of mothers selected for the purpose but, in keeping with Calvert's muddled life and crazed repertoire, there was no proof.

The result was that, found guilty of the murder, the death sentence was passed.

A Leeds City Councillor said at the time that he felt pity for her and added: 'She was a thin, wan-looking creature only weighing a few stone. I should never legislate on the lines of hanging a woman.' But others soon realised that there were two Louie Calverts. In the dock she had been quiet, restrained and polite but down in the cell she shouted abuse at her husband, trying to say that he was to blame. All he could say was: 'It can't be helped lass.'

Other interpretations of her actions and responses to graphic descriptions of the attack on Waterhouse and of the corpse in court indicated that she was unfeeling and mentally distant from any sense of the events unfolding being real.

But the woman who was seen as undersized and pathetic had apparently done the awful deed, proven to be wily and cunning in the extreme. Her actions in court and before the magistrate when first charged show an amount of guile too. She dressed in dark colours and to the local reporters became 'the woman in black.' It has been noted that she fussed over her appearance as if she were still putting on clothes to be someone else, to project a persona which was not really her. In the magistrate's court, even as evidence was being spoken, she changed her hat, putting on a black silk one instead of her everyday mauve.

There was an appeal held in London. She was again dressed all in black and the context at the time was a sensitive one with regard to the hanging of women. Since the notorious Edith Thompson case in 1923, who had been found guilty of conspiracy – of foreknowledge and incitement of the murder of her husband by her lover but not the deed itself – and hanged, the eight women given a death sentence afterwards had all been reprieved. It was assumed by many that this was going to be the case again with Calvert, as a petition had been signed by 3,000 people. Much was made in the press on the topic of her recently acquired child and the question of what would happen to her and who might adopt the infant was something that sold papers.

But a major factor considered in the appeal was that she was not pregnant as claimed.

There was also nothing new evidentially and, in spite of the media interest in the case and in the very emotive issue of hanging a woman, the sentence was not quashed. Relatives came to pay a last visit to her in the cell and Louie wrote a letter on her last night on earth and in it said, 'I am keeping up quite well and you will have the joy of meeting me in heaven, for I am quite ready and prepared to meet my God.'

Finally, this enigmatic woman who had fuelled her life on lies, confessed the crime to the warders and also said, after clearly being troubled by something that was on her conscience, that she had murdered another victim – an old man she used to work for as his housekeeper. It would be easy to argue that this was a lie, too; that she was again fantasising. If she did kill Frobisher, there must have been a way to overcome the obvious obstacle of how could such a tiny woman have conveyed the corpse to the river. Louie Calvert was said to have gone to her death, 'more bravely than many men.' There was an element of Louie Calvert which had that essence of brutal, unfeeling detachment we see in serial killers, but very rarely in women.

This is a tale embedded in a very familiar template. It has the inevitable narrative arc of the women-killer that runs through British history: a desperate and poor woman, someone from the streets, dirty and immoral, takes the life of a tiny, weak woman, for money. She is arrested and charged, investigations begin into her life, relationships and background. But everything points to her as the killer. Then in court, she is advised not to speak. Although that right has been allowed in British criminal law since 1898, her counsel feel that her own testimony would go against her. After all, she is a woman of ill repute, and worse, she looks strange – and what's all this about her love of keeping the boots of her victims? No, the female is more deadly than the male. She is condemned, and is to hang. The clamour for a reprieve begins but the law takes its course and she mounts the scaffold and meets her maker.

The place to begin is with Louie herself and Leeds at this time. In November, 1925, the Home Secretary, Mr Joynson-Hicks, was asked to do something about the growing menace of prostitution. His response was reported in *The Times*.

'He was speaking as a man, and he supposed there was no man who had not been solicited. He thought their feelings were pity and sorrow, and he thought they would find very few men who would go into the witness box and condemn those unfortunate women. At the same time, he believed it was his duty to try to get those women off the streets... If he set up a departmental committee he could appoint a Lord Justice of Appeal to preside...'

That was not going to help anyone and it missed the point that prostitution almost always equated with desperation and poverty. In 1925, as the po-faced politicians discussed the problem, around central Leeds – from the Parish Church to the Calls, and to Leeds Bridge and the viaducts – it was a thriving trade, and two who lived by it were Lily Waterhouse and Louie Calvert.

I started this account of Louie by imagining her in Strangeways prison, awaiting her execution and writing her life in an exercise book. Now let's retrace her life back to October that year, when she left her husband at their home in Pottery Fields, Hunslet, ostensibly to go and have her child in Dewsbury. Arty, not the most observant or caring of men, clearly had no idea about women's lives and bodies. With her adopted baby, Louie then set about finding a home.

The Chief Constable of Leeds provided a profile of Louie for the Home Office. He wrote that she was 30 (in May, 1926) and, 'Had been leading a life of crime since 1911, her name then being Gomersall.'

His report confirmed that at that time of arrest she had two illegitimate children: Annie, aged nine, was in the Dewsbury Union Cottage Home, and Kenneth was living with Arty in Hunslet. The police chief added, 'Since her discharge from prison on or about 3 June, 1922 she has worked at Messrs Boyes and Helliwells, Bramley... as a weaver for a few months in 1924... She has also worked at Messrs Womersley, Waterloo Mills, Pudsey, and in both cases was discharged owing to her being a very unsatisfactory worker and time-keeper.' We know little of her family, except that her father was a railway worker.

Louie had lived with a John Frobisher, in Mary Street, West End, and this man had, according to a coroner's verdict, committed suicide on 14th July, 1922. This was to come back into Louie's life later. What then happened from October, 1926, was that Lily Waterhouse and Louie lived together, on the game. We have the most detailed account of this time, right up to Lily's death, from Leeds bookseller, William Byrne. His business was at 19, Park Lane, so he was placed ideally for Louie's movement between Hunslet and New Wortley. Lily came to his shop and spun a tale about a man owing her money and that she was in dire straits. Byrne was a kind gentleman who recalled: 'I was sorry for the woman and I continued to give her food each day when she came to my shop, until the end of December, 1925. I knew that she was getting in arrears with her rent... I was not satisfied with her habits. I found that she was dirty and I advised her to find work. I could not keep her in food any longer. From October to December she was at my shop practically the whole day and ran errands for me...'

Her visits became less frequent and then in early May she arrived with Louie Calvert. The two women – both around the same age and five feet tall – laughed and joked in Byrne's company, and Louie said she was married but estranged from her husband. She had obviously left Arty to have an adventure, and that aspect of her – running away to indulge in a fantasy life – is central to her personality.

Lily came again and told Byrne that she and Louie were happy together and one time she explained that she had left Louie at home looking after the house.

On 27th March we have some interesting information about Lily Waterhouse. She asked Byrne for half a crown so she could go to hospital to have a sulphur bath. That meant that she had 'the itch' – scabies, a disease of poverty and poor hygiene. But there was more – she had a deformity, and Byrne refers to this as entailing the wearing of, 'shoulder steels or irons for this complaint and she showed me a portion of these last Friday, 26th March.' She almost certainly had what is now known as Sprengel's 'dropped shoulder.' The poor woman, as she reported to Byrne, said that at the hospital the staff had damaged her irons, the brace she wore to keep her dropped shoulder in place. Sprengel's shoulder can affect the spine and also the neck, commonly making the neck barely defined and difficult to see.

Then the whole story of Lily and Louie turns sour.

Lily went to tell her confidant and friend Byrne that Louie was stealing from her and that she was also frightened of her. Lily had found pawn tickets in a bag and they were made out in her name although Louie had gone to pawn the items. Byrne advised her to go to the Town Hall and see a magistrate, thus starting a process of police action. She told Byrne later that she had an appointment at the Town Hall on the 31st March in the morning. Lily, as Byrne reported, spoke of being afraid. 'She said Louie had said, 'If I set about you, you are a cripple, and it will hurt you." Lily looked very worried and told him: "I will catch the 9.30 car [tramcar] in the morning.' Lily then left my shop and returned again about four and came again on 31st and said: 'I have been to the magistrates and they have told me to secure the other pawn tickets, they advise me to send Louie away to the pictures and get the tickets while she is away... I am very sorry that Louie has been so unkind to me...' Byrne never saw her again. The last thing he did for her was make her a cup of tea.

When Lily did not return to the Town Hall on the

appointed hour, the police started to be concerned and two officers were sent to her house. Detective John Holland went to the address and in his report he gives the first account of what became a murder scene. This was on the 1st of April, and Holland asked around about potential goings on. He was told that: 'The woman lodger had left the house carrying a baby about 8.30pm the previous night and she (the lodger) informed Mrs Clayton, a neighbour, that she had left Mrs Waterhouse in bed, crying, because she was leaving her.'

Holland had a key from a Mrs Button, another neighbour, and when he reached the small bedroom, he made notes of the scene.

'We noticed the body of Mrs Waterhouse lying on the floor on her right side and found that she was dead... Her shoulders and head were resting on a small, square mattress, her legs and feet resting on a similar mattress, with her feet towards the window. Her hands were clenched and the wrists were crossed and resting on the lower part of the body, with her knees slightly drawn up. We then noticed that there was a mark on her neck, also marks on her wrists. She was fully dressed with the exception of her hat and boots. Lying across her feet was a piece of string, another piece was close to it. Behind the body was a piece of tape and on an orange box was a belt of similar material to the coat that the woman had on. These were taken possession of.' The last sentence is very important. The detective took the coat belt. Later, the medical inspection, by the surgeon Dr Hoyland Smith, concluded that she had dying by strangulation, but there was no item known that could have been used. His report mentions a half-inch stretch of a mark, as part of the marks made by the strangling – just right for a coat belt.

The next day, D.S. Sabey and D.C. Chester went to arrest Louie at the Calvert home in Railway Place, Pottery

Fields. She told them she had been at the Waterhouse place the night before. As she walked out with the officers, Louie asked what this was all about, and asked: 'Has she done herself in?'

When Sabey went back to search the address at Railway Place, he reported that he found a suitcase containing clothes and materials, some of them with the name 'Waterhouse' stitched on. Later, the police returned to search further and found crockery, some scarves and other items. Arty said he had never seen them before. Two theatre programmes were seized, with the name Waterhouse written in. Louie Calvert was now the only suspect. The case put together was that she had approached Lily in Bond Street, asking about lodgings. Lily took her in and they began something of an adventure together – going to meet other women under one of the central Leeds viaducts when looking for male custom. The investigation became fixated with the fact that boots had been taken and evidence of them being pawned by Louie was found – they earned her four shillings and sixpence.

A great deal depended on a proper forensic report from Dr Hoyland Smith now. He went to the murder scene in the early afternoon and wrote a note to the Chief Constable saying that death had been by violence and that it had occurred between 12 to 24 hours previously. That's a very big window and we know that Louie was seen leaving at 8.30 pm – over 16 hours before Smith arrived. He then did a full autopsy which was completed by 7th April and in that he summarised his and Dr Taylor's findings. There was a deep pressure mark around the neck, with the width of a half inch. The hair on the back part of the scalp was matted with blood. The body was covered in bruises, particularly on the shoulder and hip, with more on the legs. But what Smith failed to mention was the deformity and the steel shoulder brace. There was 'an effusion of blood, the size of a shilling on the left side, over the parietal bone. In the neighbourhood of the occipital protuberance was a penetrating wound of the scalp extending down to the pericranium... less than a half inch in length and bled profusely... death had occurred from strangulation.'

There had been a struggle then. In fact, the wound described which would have floored the victim was low under the downward curve of the lamdoid suture. Whatever instrument had been used to make that would have had to be applied from below, either when the victim was lying on her front with her head turned downwards, or applied from lower behind, in the movement of an uppercut. None of this was theorized at the time. Forensic examination was not so detailed and streamlined as it is now. The crucial point is that the occipital protuberance is underneath the back of the skull. A later report said that there was blood on the wall also, and that adds to the extreme doubt here that a tiny woman such as Louie could have managed to fight Lily and hit her beneath the lower back of the skull, and still have such an attack linked to blood on the wall. The blood could only have come from the entry of some tool into the skull. There was no source of blood flow anywhere else. Also, the bed which Louie said had been occupied by Lily before she left was unused and actually covered in dust.

When Hoyland Smith added further notes on the victim, we learn much more. He thought that a blunt instrument had been used all over the body, and twice on the head. He noted that there was no venereal disease and he thought that the wrists had been tied. Most significantly, Smith wrote, 'The strangulation could not have been caused by the string or the tape as the pressure was much too wide for either.' Everyone had forgotten about the belt. The wrists had been tied before death and the strangulation, Smith theorised, could have been done by someone, 'of small build' as long as they got the victim in a certain position. That would have involved a great deal of lifting and struggling for a very small woman such as Louie. Smith stated that he was sure there had been, 'a prolonged struggle.'

This all points to someone bigger and stronger being able to move, push or even carry Lily's body to the floor where she was found. Oddly, the belt, which was almost certainly used and taken away by the police was never mentioned again. It seems ever more highly likely that there was someone else involved, and when D.S. Pass went to interview Louie when she was in custody on 2nd April, we have this. 'She said that Lily was expecting a man named Fred Crabtree to come and stay with her that night. I asked who Crabtree was. She said he was an ex-soldier from Beckett Park Hospital who is going to Canada on Saturday, and that Crabtree had been there last Sunday and stayed all night. I asked her how many keys there were to the house and she said, 'Three, Lily had one, I had one, and Crabtree had one.' Louie added that the intended bed had been put up because Lily was afraid of a police raid. At the time, any suspicion of an actual brothel would be subject to scrutiny and to raids. Louie's comments seem to make sense.

What sort of woman are we dealing with when we consider the victim?

Lily Waterhouse, clearly living with pain and having to put up with the steel shoulder brace, was the same height as Louie, just five feet tall. She was undernourished, having had to rely on Mr Byrne's charity to keep something in her stomach; she had been desperate enough to walk 'under the dark arches' to look for customers and that would have meant 'knee tremblers' more often than men taken home. When she went to see the police about Louie, D.C. Watson, who made notes on the interview, recorded that, 'She had reason to believe that a woman lodger named Louie whose surname she was unable to remember had pledged three articles...' Lily was frail, also suffering from scabies and, as seen by Dr Smith, had bruises over her body. The important point here is that she and Louie had lived and laughed and been on the game together for six months. As they were always in dire necessity when it came to the basics of survival, it seems that Louie's statement that the visits to the pawnbrokers were a joint decision, as money was in short supply, is at least plausible. Also, if money was indeed Louie's motive, why was so much in the house at Amberley Road when the body was found? There were small amounts in various receptacles and even a ten shilling note in a box...

I would suggest that we need to look more closely at Fred Crabtree. The Leeds police certainly did initially. Inspector Winstanley, Assistant Chief Constable in Liverpool, wrote to his Leeds counterpart on 7th April, to report that in response to their telephone call about Crabtree, that passenger manifests had been checked and that, 'Should Crabtree attempt to leave the country through this port, the necessary action will be taken, or in the event of obtaining any information which will lead to tracing his whereabouts... a further report will be submitted.'

Before that call to Liverpool, the local police had tracked down Crabtree. He made a statement on the 6th April, claiming he had travelled from Barnsley to Becketts Park to have treatment on his eye (he was hit by gun-shot in the war when he was in the Barnsley Pals). If the call was made to Liverpool the next day, where had he gone, what did they need to corroborate and why could they not contact him again? The truth is that he disappears after this interview. In a long statement he gives a very full and detailed account of his movements and what is particularly strange is that a whole batch of other statements, made by family members and friends, read in exactly the same way. One might almost think that they had been briefed on what to say. Studying them all in one sitting leads to the conclusion that someone wanted there to be a firm alibi, particularly for a wound on Crabtree's face.

It seems highly likely that Fred Crabtree did call on Lily and Louie, in need of female company and sex. If the Crabtree who was allegedly in the fight at Amberley Road was the Fred Crabtree from Barnsley, we need to revisit his statement given on the 6th April. Becketts Park hospital confirmed that Fred had attended for treatment on the 30th March, so he could have gone to Amberley Road after that and stayed for a few nights, leaving after killing Lily. In his statement he is meticulous about times and events. A very important note is that he says that on 1st April, there was a fall from the roof at the mine where he worked. This allegedly hit him in the eye which caused a swelling. The son of the Rising Son pub's licensee told the police, 'I noticed that his right eye was swollen and I asked him what he had done to his eye... he replied, "I've got a bat on it at work." He was referring to a pit prop which had fallen, before the roof caved in according to one witness.

Louie's perspective is detailed in her prison notebook. It read, '... last Sunday I was there this woman brought a man home supposed to be a soldier from Becketts Park hospital for wounded soldiers and after he had been there a few days we began to quarrel about him – she wanted him and he wanted me but I wanted neither. I wanted to leave them and go home as it was beginning to get a bit too hot... the detectives were on our tracks and we could not go out without them pulling up... Well on the Wednesday night, the day I was going to leave her, we went out and had a few drinks with this man... we all started to quarrel and it got to fighting... oh the drink...he said something nasty to her and she landed out with her fist to him and they both rolled on the floor... when she got up and struck out again, I picked up the poker... my intention was to strike the man and make him leave off hitting her...' Louie adds to this that as she swung the poker, Crabtree dodged out of the way and the poker struck Lily. Louie then said that Crabtree 'went mad' and took a belt and strangled her. That coat belt was the nearest to hand and was left there, as the detective noted when he came and found the body. At the trial at Leeds Assizes, Louie did not speak. Since 1898 there had been legislation that allowed, for the first time, the accused to make a statement. Most criminal defence lawyers preferred their clients not to as, in virtually all cases, the accused would say something that would incriminate them or, at least, be legally naive in terms of understanding how to 'play' in the court drama.

The press report on the trial stated, 'The appellant, a young woman dressed in black, appeared in the custody of two wardresses.'

That is all that is said about Louie apart from, 'She was a frail-looking married woman.' She was never asked a question but stood, a silent witness. The timid woman before the jury was supposed to have wrestled with Lily, hit her with a blunt instrument before tying her wrists and feet and then strangled her. The poker, we assume was taken away by Louie. It was not mentioned again in the prison notebook.

We now also know that Louie's husband Arty, was a violent man. He had battered his wife and children and had been given three months in prison for an assault on their son,

Kenneth. It seems more than likely that when Louie ran away to have what seemed to police at the time as her 'adventures', she was actually having a respite from violence and domestic abuse.

At the inquest, before the assizes, the possibility of there being two people involved in the death of Lily Waterhouse was raised. The coroner wanted to know from Dr Smith if such a scenario was likely given the nature of the attack. Smith said one person could do it but, 'All depended on the position in which the woman was seized.' There was no more close scrutiny given. No mention was made of the main wound being under the base of the skull.

Louie, if acting alone, would have had to move the body around several times. Such a scenario is highly unlikely. This all makes Louie's prison notebook remarks all the more believable and the same applies to the death of her previous employer, Mr Frobisher. Louie wrote, 'He came home drunk and behaving in a disgusting manner and using foul language in front of the baby and when I told him to stop it he struck me... when I started fighting back and struck him a foul blow which caused him to fall down the cellar steps and break his neck... it was brought in as accidental death.'

Before the trial, the police had followed up Louie's previous life and they began to suspect that she was a fantasist who had travelled across the land gaining domestic positions and then robbing her employers. Also, the fact that boots were missing in both of the deaths linked to her, led to explanations of her as a fetishist. In fact, the truth is far more mundane.

In the pawnshop, a pair brought a useful sum in 1926. In broadcasting information about her, there was an interesting response from London. A Mr Owen responded in a letter saying that he suspected a Miss Calvert who had married him in London, to have been Louie. But on being shown a photo, he wrote again, 'I am now satisfied that the prisoner is not the woman I married.' The reason that the Leeds police chased up these leads is that it had now been confirmed that between 1920 and 1925, Louie had worked as a live-in housekeeper for several men, one of whom had been the father of Kenneth – James Jackson, who was then in the army in India.

Why would Louie have spun any kind of web of lies? She was condemned. To her friends on their last visit to her she asserted her innocence, at least with regard to the murder charge. At the appeal court, when the last attempt to save her life failed, her lawyer argued that there had been inadmissible evidence from the senior detective. The *Yorkshire Post* report explained. 'Her Counsel, Mr E.C. Chappell, said the grounds of appeal were that the evidence of a detective superintendent at the trial was not admissible, because it was admitted by this witness that for several hours before being charged the appellant was examined and cross-examined by him. The cross-examination, it was submitted, was carried to 'an unprecedented degree.'

There was also more detail given about the statements made by neighbours on the evening of the killing. Dr Smith now stated that the noises heard from the bedroom probably lasted from one to two minutes, rather than for ten to fifteen minutes, as previously thought, and also he now made a more specific statement about the time of death, putting it between nine at night and five the next morning. Louie left the premises at 8.30.

Arty Calvert took part in an appeal for a reprieve. The *Yorkshire Evening Post* reported on 16th June, 'The reply was not favourable and we are now driven to this petition as a last resort. The centuries-old law regarding a convicted woman murderer is not held to apply in this case, in spite of the supporting evidence given by Dr Hoyland Smith.' The reference here is to her health and particularly to her alleged pregnancy. Smith seems to have at first thought she was pregnant but then changed his mind.

Louie was hanged at Strangeways on 24th June. The press described the scene. 'She gave no trouble to the executioner, Pierrepoint, and his two assistants, and her conduct generally was in keeping with her behaviour in the prison itself.'

As a crime writer and historian of well-tried experience in murder cases, I am left with a very likely scenario of that fateful night in Amberley Road. Fred Crabtree had come after his hospital appointment. He had told his workmates that he had a lady-friend and he gave the alibi to those in the pub. He went out drinking with the women and when they came home, the fight began. He was a strong man, being a coal-miner. He it was who had the muscle-power required to overcome little Lily in the scrap. Louie, despite her stature, tried to take extreme action to stop the man from killing her housemate. The hammer hit Lily under the skull because Fred, dodging out of the way, would have been behind the victim, attempting to strangle her. The hammer would then have hit Lily in the place defined by Dr Hoyland Smith. The blood spurted up the wall. Fred tied up his victim, who was not yet dead. He wanted his kicks. The strangulation came when the victim was hog-tied. He then ran off. The place had been watched by the police anyway, as a den of vice. There would be panic. Louie was now hiding, probably locking herself in the other bedroom. Fred left with a black eye.

Louie was left alone. She untied her dead friend and then placed her with her head on the pillow. She must then have left in fear as there was nothing else stolen. When the neighbour spoke with her, Louie said that Lily was in bed, crying. She was planting a seed that would flourish into an explanation. That is why she asked the police if Lily had done herself in. The case has been studied by Annette Ballinger, an academic criminologist and she concludes that there had been a process of 'truth production' by the official forces who sustained the bias of the criminal trial process and police investigation. Louie's account, written in prison, was not believed and in fact taken as an admission of guilt.

As a coda to Louie's story, it should be pointed out that the police looked fairly deeply into Crabtree and for incidents with a similar modus operandi and in a given location regarding the suspect. In this case, they found such a murder, in Sheffield. Just a few months before the Waterhouse killing, on 27th January, 1926, the body of Florence Hargreaves was found at her shop in 697 Attercliffe Road. She had a small drapery business and lived alone. The police issued a wanted poster and gave a description of how she had died. 'When the body was found it was dressed; a stocking was tied tightly round the neck, and death was due to strangulation preceded by injuries to the head and chest (fractured ribs).'

This case remains unsolved although, the Sheffield police saw the similarities in this case and that of Lily Waterhouse. Further details, supplied by Dr Godfrey Carter at the inquest on Miss Hargreaves, show the similarities in more detail. 'There was blood upon both hands... Round the neck a tight ligature was tied in a knot at the back. It was about half an inch in breadth. It was found to be a long cotton stocking... There were bruises on the left eye. On the left side of the scalp and the dome of the skull high above the ear was a jagged wound extending down to the bone... At the back of the head was a vertical wound three quarters of an inch in length penetrating to the covering of the bone...'

There are marked comparisons, notably the nature of the strangling and the positioning of the wound to the left. Oddly, in this case, the doctor thought that there was no indication of a struggle. But there was almost certainly no other person present, as there was when Louie allegedly intervened. Although there was nothing conclusive, the Hargreaves murder does provide supporting information. When the under secretary at the Home Office was informed, he was of the opinion that there were two different Crabtree's and his opinion was accepted.

In my case file, I have a police fingerprint sheet with Louie's daubs on it and there is a box in one corner where a brief description of her is written. She was five feet tall with brown hair and had a mole on the right side of her nose. She was born in 1896 and when she was remanded was 30 years old but seemingly having already packed into them, a lifetime. The prints seem very blunt and flat at the tips and one suspects that the famous profiler and crime cataloguer, Alphonse Bertillon, back in the 1890s, would have had a ready-made definition of what 'type' she was – maybe bantam weight, a fighting sparrow. My file of police reports has a musty smell, mirroring the countless hours spent on the papers by the Leeds detectives, soaked in tobacco, sweat and boredom.

Writing about women killers turned out to be upsetting in many ways.

The more I researched cases, the more I felt that British history and its criminal law in the eighteenth and nineteenth centuries was horrendously brutal towards them, in every conceivable way. Often the word 'infanticide' cropped up and the less inclined was I to write the story and call it murder. Of course, there was an intention to kill but the notion of mitigating medical factors did not exist until around 1920.

Some of the most notorious cases of women being tried for wilful murder in English history involve moral beliefs and ideologies of power that are impossible to accept today.

Something profound in the human mind and in the sense of moral community feels an extraordinary revolt at the thought of a woman taking a life. When she did so of her husband, until 1827, a woman was not committing murder but petty treason and that meant a punishment of burning at the stake up to 1790. When a woman was hanged for husband murder, even as late as 1825 the ritual in the official execution was very different from that of a male killer, as this account of the death of Hannah Read in Leicester shows.

'A bed or mattress was placed upon the sledge, which was drawn by a horse, upon which the prisoner was secured by a rope. On reaching the Bridewell, she was carried into the gaoler's house... About eleven o'clock she was again placed upon the sledge, and was drawn along the gaol yard to the foot of the steps leading to the scaffold; soon after she appeared on the platform followed by the High Sheriff and the usual attendants... She seemed earnest in supplicating mercy for her sins and invoking the divine favour on her unfortunate children and relatives...' (*The Times* 9th August 1825)

Hannah Read had a very different experience from that of the average male murderer. Her crime, murder of an abusive husband, was nonetheless deemed a more extreme form of sin and a more outrageous offence against the social and religious hierarchy.

The press reports of the alarmingly common cases of attempted suicide and infanticide are desperately sad, as in this typical one from 1850. 'Mary Hardwick, a miserable–looking creature, was indicted for attempting to murder her child. On the Saturday proceeding she was seen standing with a child in her arms near the Brighton custom-house, when she suddenly ran down to the sea, threw the child into the water, and then jumped in herself. The woman and child were dragged out in a state of insensibility...' When the poor woman recovered, her husband reviled her and, 'Expressed a wish that she had drowned herself.' The phrase 'murder her child' was in italics in this report from Dickens's journal, *Household Narrative*. In the Victorian period, this kind of tragic attempt at suicide was counterbalanced in the unsound morality of the time with the case of affiliation. That is, attempts to kill the children of immoral unions in order to avoid being a 'fallen women' were rife; but what about the male transgressors?

A case from Dewsbury in 1850 shows this, as here a man of the cloth, Rev. Stephen Matthews, was in the dock. This vicar of Hanging Heaton stood accused of being the father of an illegitimate child born to Mary Hellewell who was 16 years old. The court now found, as this was a retrial, that, 'Criminal intercourse had continued for two years.' Nevertheless, the magistrates declined to make an order of affiliation, which would have tied the churchman to a regular maintenance payment for the upkeep and education of his child. These affiliation hearings were rare.

In most instances, the chosen means of murder by women was poison.

In 1850 a report on the number of people tried for murder by such in the years 1839-1849 recorded 154. Of these, 69 were men and 85 by the hands of women. The notorious nineteenth century cases of Florence Maybrick in Liverpool and Priscilla Biggadyke in Lincolnshire, together with the mystery of Florence Bravo, have made the poison narrative familiar to true crime readers, typically against the backdrop of adulterous love or revenge after maltreatment. In working class households, this was often in terms of arsenic being soaked from fly-papers. But these poison stories and women killers are always complicated by the popularity of arsenic and other poisons being taken in very small doses by men, with the aim of enhancing their sexual potency. James Maybrick in Liverpool (once a Ripper suspect) was one such addict. Louie Calvert's tale appears to be one of injustice fed upon ingrained prejudice.

6

•

TIMES
BEHIND BARS

My learning curve as a crime writer received its greatest boost after a spell in residence in a number of detention centres of Her Majesty's pleasure. Now, after reading so much about killers, I met a number, and wrote stories with them.

It came as no surprise to learn that very few of them were deranged homicidal maniacs. Most were sons, fathers, mothers, daughters, brothers, sons – attached to family and, in most aspects of their lives, as undistinguished as the man on the Clapham omnibus. There were exceptions and they are a challenge when it comes to figuring out why they killed. People have murdered over a wrong word spoken in haste or in a frenzy of twisted jealousy. Very few take pleasure in the craft of killing.

In prison, cons are strangely transmuted into shadows of the people whose faces plagued police appeals and local newspaper features. Outside, they may have been dangerous to know but inside, they only suggest something like the Homeric idea of Hades. Some even cultivate a new character they wish to project other than a standard identity number and case file. Others are trapped in this flux of life, whilst a few are, as it were, frozen, somehow outside time. It sometimes feels as if the prison itself is in a time-warp, and stepping through the gate into the wings and halls presents an experience of a bygone age.

Looking into crime – both past and present – inevitably means knowing something about prison and about life behind the bars. Through my growing up in Leeds, the huge, imposing shadow of Armley jail had been as much a skyline presence as the Brotherton Library. These were and still are, iconic signifiers of what the city has been identified with. Just as 'gone to Wakefield' always meant put behind the bars of the ancient prison there, which goes back to a Tudor workhouse and bridewell, 'gone to Armley' had a similar resonance in my part of West Yorkshire. But for a crime writer, actually mixing in with the life of the convicted provides the perfect research.

I was working with what is now the Writers in Prison Foundation. This is a wonderful organisation headed by Pauline and Clive Hopwood and provides residencies up and down the land in which writers spend time inside attempting to be cultural initiators. I joined the ranks of those strange souls who wander around wings and landings touting for inmates who might be interested in running a drama group, storytelling, writing their autobiography, having poetry readings, producing a magazine and so on – anything word-related and an artistic outlet amongst the drudgery.

I did it for six years, four of them with men and two among incarcerated women. I'd had a taste of prison before, when I gave a poetry reading in the high security jail at Full Sutton, near York, with poet Bernard Young back in 1990. We read our poems and the audience of killers and terrorist suspects were very attentive. They asked lots of intelligent questions and showed us a marvellous literary magazine they produced inside. It also turned out they were all better read than me. It was a very rewarding experience and well worth running the gauntlet of various savage dogs which were stationed at doorways on the way in.

But then came my residencies, and the first memory of one of the early experiences is not for the faint-hearted. I had been working in the chapel with a drama group. It was November and by that time in the evening it was very dark. The room I had been in was next to the library, on the edge of a huge parade ground, as the place had once been a military base, some years before. I had to walk about 50 yards to the office assigned to me in the library when suddenly the bell sounded for all prisoners wandering around on association to return to their wings for roll-call. There was a gang of half-a-dozen men outside the library, and they were clearly not shifting. They were laughing and telling jokes. Then they saw me. Something inside me told me that I had to just carry on, walk up to them, but avoid opening any doors in case they might exploit that few seconds of opportunity.

There were no officers in sight. In seconds, I weighed the situation. I had keys on my belt and if they got hold of them they could have hauled me into a room and there could be a hostage situation. It is strange how the mind enacts these scenarios so quickly. Maybe I'd seen too many thrillers. What I did was to say hello and smile. They were East Europeans and the first thing they talked about was how one of them was in for a knife attack. They all enjoyed teasing him about his handiwork with a blade. Hardly comforting, you might think. But the thing is, I felt instinctively that anything else but a relaxed mood would not be right. I asked about their countries of origin, their backgrounds. They responded. What was, maybe, three minutes seemed like an hour.

Somehow, we all laughed. I can't even recall what I said that amused them but I told some kind of story, showed an interest in them, an eccentric Brit in a dark space in between their cell block and a pile of books. They moved away, back towards their wing. I carried on according to routine, opening the library door and going to my office. It was only later that night that I realised the risk involved. I had a whistle on my belt, no radio, and I could have blown it just to cover myself. That would have brought somebody, although maybe too late. What it brought home was the vulnerability that all prison staff are subject to.

This is the nature of a prison though, and always has been. The few control the many.

The operative discipline occurs because of what individuals have to lose which outweighs what they have to gain. In a prison regime, the logistics minimise the opportunities and in most cases the human traffic and the interplay of empowered and dispossessed works, a holding operation based on mind games and convention. The scariest moments happen when there is a possibility that the animal pack can act; that happens when the odds are suddenly out of kilter. But even then, there is a high risk for any who thinks of transgressing.

Out of town, well away from the law-abiding, the prison stands as a red-brick fortress, with high walls surmounted by bizarre, rounded black tops, reminiscent of some eastern castle. Around it there is the suburban normality: little avenues and crescents, a playing field and on one long side, a tract of no man's land. Behind the walls there are wings stretching out from a central observation tower, with offices and assorted huts for various specialists dotted around. Every day, arriving in the car park and seeing the high, formidable walls, a slight frisson of fear runs through you. Without that, you would be vulnerable.

Within the walls there are those who made errors of judgement or took fecklessness to lawless dimensions. Others with mental problems and those with no ability to control anger. Several who want to forget the world and other people, and bizarrely to most of us, some who see the place, strangely, as home. There, on return, they meet old friends and tell tales of small offences and sad transgressions. Then watching them every minute of the day, there are the officers, vigilant, bored, oppressed, with the patience of Job and usually drained of all optimism that prison will ever 'work' – whatever that means.

I, along with all other staff, enter through the massive gate, queuing to collect my keys for the belt. I show my I.D., and patiently wait for movement. Anything could happen at any time to stop it. Outside the gate there is a designated 'frozen' area – stark, uninhabited, there simply for traffic of all kinds, human and motorized, to pass through. It's officially known as a 'sterile area' and that term always raises questions in newcomers. Then, through gate after gate, with the drill of unlock, look behind, lock, walk on to the next one. You pray that your over-used key will not one day snap in the lock. Should that happen you stand still, call for assistance, wait like a statue, for security to be put into motion.

The working day for the writer in residence begins, sorting through my diary and looking at piles of paper, messages and official requests. Then decisions as to which

113

wing or place I should visit first. I worked anywhere I wanted, so I could see a man in the gym, the workshops, the laundry, education rooms, reception, health care, one of the many huts or even in the kitchens, where I would have a writers' meeting squashed between huge ovens and various vats or vibrating machines whose function was unknown to me. In the first months, it was a case of learning the geography and that meant working out the transit from one place to another. In a prison there are so many doors that it's like some fairground hall of mirrors in its level of confusion. For a year I took the longest possible route to one area, then one day realised that there was a door which admitted me to the usual destination in about 30 seconds.

A typical day included one-to-one talks, poetry workshops, storytelling sessions, drama work, magazine editorial meetings and office work. The job is all about forging relationships and I was there to work with officers and all other staff on their writing skills, as well as with the prisoners. The clerical workers, sports hall staff, maintenance workers, canteen people, probation officers and countless other people are also guests of Her Majesty, just that they can go home after their shift. Atypical events were startling and over the first few months I had a taste of many. One thankfully fairly rare event is when a bell goes on a wing and within seconds there is a rush of medical staff towards a cell – often they arrive to see a body swinging – yet on most occasions, they save a life. Prisons have so many unsung heroes.

This work place is grand, horrendous, hilarious, tragic beyond belief, impressive, frustrating, farcical, pungent, out-dated, essential, frightening and comforting, all at once. For the writer in residence, the most typical scene is a conversation in a cell possibly about a personal tragedy or how to scan a sonnet, such diversity sums up the environment. Or talks on subjects such as coping with the death of someone on the outside, the nature of innocence, making money from writing, the varying characters of the staff – all great source material. In between all of that we write. How is success measured for me as a writer placed on the inside? In one sense, it's what pleases the Governor: magazines, booklets, performances, a reduction in pent-up aggression maybe. Having some arty type wandering around trying to start a book club is also good for the public image and useful when external inspections take place. But I have to say that all the Governors I have worked with, except in one case, were genuinely interested in my work.

When you go home from this strange workplace, you think of those left in, padded up with someone they have to learn to like. And when I used to go out in the dusk after a drama workshop, I considered the guys lying in bed, tortured by thoughts of home and of wives, dreaming of the wonders of simplicity – being able to cook a meal, watch a film, plant potatoes, kiss your son or daughter... And then I used to look at the skyline of this absurd concept, towers and chapel roof against a red sky, lines of wings and walls with late sun glossing the bricks, shouts and songs from the pads, and I used to sense the sympathy ebbing away as I recalled the infinite number of victims, both of the crime and left in the aftermath of it. Those on the outside, wrecked personalities washed up on the shores of perplexity and confusion, trying to understand what has happened to shake their lives, what storm had been and gone. Human wrecks who have sobbed, become strangers to sleep, illusions shattered, put lives on hold, lost direction and maybe most of the words they used to comfort themselves and their loved ones with in what was a life of a different routine.

Murder in Mind

At prison visiting time, I saw the other victims in glimpses, partners and families, mums and dads; ordinary, frail, brimming with the human banality and plainness we all have when at the mercy of others and 'the system', as well as with obvious love and caring. Those men and women in classes and cells were suddenly rich in deeper lives, more complex identities. Amongst such a backdrop, one of the initial issues for the writer is to get noticed amongst the drab, humdrum, highly regimented existence of the institution. Initially, I designed flyers claiming, 'Your imagination has no cell!' and 'Set your words free!' It's hard to strike that initial note of recognition. In hindsight, what I should have done is, perhaps, plunge over the rail on a wing into the anti-suicide net and started reading a poem.

I was very low profile. When they trooped into the classrooms for in many cases initially undesired education, I was there, like a spare part, ready to inspire them out of torpor, to offer at least in the short time we were together, a form of escapism, if only of the imagination. I worked on writing with several members of staff and I think they began to understand what I was doing there.

Despite being usually based in the library, I always felt transient. In one jail my base was changed four times, shrinking with each move but, to all intents and purposes, I didn't matter. Appearance is important. Advice to the writer is normally that a colour contrasting with the prisoners' apparel is best but loud and dazzling clothes are best avoided. I opted for khaki, with a purple shirt beneath and nondescript trousers. The main point was that I wanted to be noticed, but not so that fingers would point and there would be ridicule. Then I came to see that ridicule was quite cool, because it meant that you were noticed

Predominantly, I bothered, nagged and pestered any

person in authority who could do something to make creative activity happen. I gradually understood that for prison staff, happiness is the closed door and no questions.

I was a nonentity in a world of buzzers, whinges, complaints, requests, orders and schedules; I was an eccentric in the midst of conformity. The presence of anything extra added on to the routine is an irritation and best ignored. The answer for me was to create a reason why my offerings would be useful, not least peace and quiet – keeping prisoners busy and productive, but that meant that I had to be trusted to do it right and not disturb the blessed stasis of an orderly wing.

In prison-speak, what I had to offer was purposeful activity. The stats demanded that as many prisoners as possible were being useful. So yes, I totted up figures and kept records and registers, but the fundamental reason I was there was to help people access words to enrich their lives, to bring about changes of thought process, to mend relationships. I had to prove that words mattered and I need not have worried. There was an implicit acknowledgement by those who knew prison life well that words were indeed at the root of most troubles.

Dig deeper into what actually happens in the lives of the prison officers in Britain today. Dwell for a moment on the sheer absurdity of starting a shift in which you put on dark trousers and a pristine white shirt, shiny and pressed like those worn by Yankee sheriffs in the cop movies, then say good morning to hundreds of men or women all shut into little boxes who have crossed a line, often through booze or drugs, and have been taken out of normality by the hand of the law.

They all end up under your roof, you bring them out, keep them busy, and then lock them in their boxes again at the end of the day. The extrapolation of the Victorian vision of the red brick radial jail: a plan to watch everyone all the time, after extracting identity and giving them a number.

For all, it is an emotional tsunami, this strange vessel called prison, adrift from love and passion, from madness and hatred into a form of belonging. This is a work place which exists with that contradiction but where talking, keeping up a dialogue, is essential. That first day I started, a young man came to me and wanted to talk. I'd run the first creative writing workshop and we had written a poem together. Then, after some encouraging grunts and an officer sweeping the class out back to their wings ready for some desultory food, the young man approached me with a wodge of paper. 'Here guv, can you read these? They're poems,' he said. 'Believe it or not, once I ran my own shop... music and that. Used to have regular customers for the wax, the old jazz E.P's and rock albums. Yeah. Then I got the other needle habit and... well, you see the results.' We looked at each other for a few seconds, then an officer reminded him that it was time to go. He was tall, spare, bald headed and with tattoos on most parts of him. He didn't smile. I had a feeling that he hadn't smiled for some time as I took his offerings.

The next day I went in search of him. I knew his name and his pad number and eventually I found him.

There was no officer in sight, so I stood there, wondering whether to open the slot and look in through his door. It seemed like a breach of his privacy. Strangely, it was relatively quiet for a minute or so, only the usual slams and shouts on some distant landing. It was silent enough in that few square feet for me to hear the sound of sobbing from behind the door. I had just decided to open the peep-hole and had my hand on the hard steel, when the sound came, gradually louder and louder. What began with a sob surging from inside his chest became a sequence of shuddering noises and I was aware that he had slithered onto the floor of the pad. I didn't ask for his door to be opened. I slipped his poems under it after writing on the top of the first sheet 'You have ability. Write more. Come and see me.'

He never did. I couldn't find him again.

Then there is the fascination with the officers' lives.

It was my third week inside the walls and I was watching, noting, listening to everything, taking in the sounds, smells and constant mutterings. An officer talked about one of the more tedious jobs.

'Bed watch is one of the most boring you can imagine. When you toddle upstairs to bed tonight, think of the poor screw sat outside the pad where a guy is on the edge. He's been slotted in there after trying to top himself and it's your job to see that his second attempt doesn't happen. The nick does that to some. They're too weak to take it. You see young lads, their brains turned to porridge with smack or crack or some shit. They start off weeping like babies in their cells. You peep in through the flap to check and they're on the floor curled up like a foetus. The severe cases are just beyond help. One of the worst was a guy who'd had sex with kith and kin and couldn't live with it when it all came out and was across the pages in the tabloids. We had to watch him like a hawk. Killing yourself is not that hard when you've got your head round it. There are guys who have done it using a cord and tap on a sink. You only need a few feet, none of this long drop stuff that the old hangmen had sussed. Drop a few feet and that can do it. So I sat there for hours, looking in. God help an officer if he's on the bed watch and the con inside manages to do the deed.'

A significant number of the prisoners are on the cusp of being sectioned. They start with self-harm and come under any banner of the term depression. The modern prison is very keen to take care of such vulnerable people. The Health Care pad is designed to cut down the risks of suicide attempts. Walking a prison now, moving from the normal wings to the sick rooms, you sense a change, the general stillness occasionally punctuated by rants or screams. The staff are impressive types; mental health in-reach workers might be a more accurate name. But the fact is that far too often, as you walk the wings, a bell goes and a gaggle of nurses dash across a landing to a pad where someone has to be cut down, pumping life back into someone who's taken all they can.

Warder 'B' is a stocky type and says that he's wrestled dozens of blokes down on the ground in his life inside. He knows a few moves and you can't get one over on him. Nothing would make his face crack, you might think. But he opens up to me about one of his worst moments.

'I was just learning the trade and there was this little fella, like a rat he was. I'd been told he had some issues. One pad mate had come to tell me that Jaz was eating himself. I joked: 'What, they've put you in with Hannibal Lector's little brother?' The truth was he had a long history of weirdness. There are some cons you just can't help. They are somewhere else, always sticking their heads into a parallel universe when normal doesn't exist. This man, he had started cutting and peeling bits of flesh off himself, mainly to upset the pad mate.

'He wants me out – he wants his own pad. Wants to be alone, boss' his fellow convict said to me. This assault on his pad mate's psyche went on. Complaints were registered. Then one night, after association they were all getting tucked up. I walked past to check on the guy as he'd been abnormally quiet and not been down to play bowls on the grass rug as usual. He was on the floor and there was a pool of blood around his head. I thought at first it was paint or muck – something in me said it couldn't be a real dead body I was looking at. But boy, he was dead. Every buzzer that could be was pressed, and there were the echoes of the nurses' feet again running along the metal floor, but all for nothing.'

'P' has spent a lot of time staring at bodies under blankets. 'You just sort of get your mind on something. Being an officer in a nick today, you spend hours bored out of your skull. When I retire, my abiding image of this work will be standing watching some Joe Soap doing something ordinary. Doing stuff in your head is the only way to survive, just keeping occupied. Who understands the human mind? Normal ones is bad enough but cons...'

If you really manage to have a talk with an officer about mental health issues the jokes will happen, like a defence mechanism, but they are just as willing to discuss how a person can be helped. One officer spoke about a young lad with severe mental health problems.

'You are sort of cushioned. You don't want to take it home with you but this lad, he was maybe 26. He used to spout poems, songs and jokes. He was the best company you could ever wish for, when he was okay. But you could go the next day and he'd be curled up sucking his thumb. You can either stand there and leave them to it, or you can do something, however small. One day I thought, what the hell, I'll tell him a story. He was rubbing his forehead against the wall and sort of sobbing. The only story I could think of was "Three Billy Goats Gruff". I read that to the grandkids the week before... He didn't move at first. He was red. It was like he'd been rubbing sandpaper across his face. He was bleeding at the neck, and I noticed that one of his finger nails was hanging off. Well I went on with the story and I thought he was not going to do anything, just go on rubbing his head.

But you know, he turned to me and a smile spread across his face... He didn't say a word, just smiled. I finished the story.'

There's also the endless patience. If there's someone in a cell requiring health care, you have to watch them all the time. It's a diligent tending of responsibility, something not normally thought of by those outside the prison wall. If they have seen *Porridge*, they might recall the one soft-hearted officer, Mr Barrowclough, who holistically cares about his charges. That character doesn't work on the front-line, instead he needs the solemn image, stony face and tough demeanour. 'P' told me: 'They come at you with questions, especially on remand. Where can I get some chocolate? I lost my phone card? The guy in my pad stinks. When can I see the vicar? That new medication don't agree with me. Sometimes it's like a stand-up patter and I crease myself. Standing and staring, that's the game. You have to watch everything. You listen hard as well.

'I got to be as keen as a cat at picking up sounds. When you're on nights, you get a rest from the staring I suppose, but boy do you listen. We have ears like bats. An officer has to be informed about so much these days, and now you're so full of information your head wants to burst. The worst is the head-counting. All day you're checking where Smith or Brown are. Who's having visits, who's moved to work in the kitchens, and who's down the block. We've got shadow boards for everything, down the workshop the cons have to use tools and there is the utmost scrutiny and logging.

'Occasionally, something like a pair of scissors will go missing and there's no movement till they're traced. The assumption is that some con wants them for a weapon... you have to make sure anything like that just will not happen...'

It soon becomes plain, after talking to prison officers, that it is a job that very few can do. One man told me that he joined the prison service after not making it as a policeman or a fireman. That gives a very negative image but part of it is about a uniform, wearing one changes your self-esteem. Put one on and you are somebody.

As 'B' put it: 'At first you've got to avoid looking in the mirror... you'll scare yourself.'

Studying or researching from prison records is not an easy task. There are barriers, many of them caused by confusion involved in the actions of the various parties who oversee them. A query from a reader of a family history magazine I wrote for regarding their ancestor who was recorded as being in Pentonville prison in 1911 led to a strenuous effort to navigate the records of a previous criminal justice system. That research will always demand a knowledge of the particular legislation and penal provision at the time. It proved almost impossible to discover why Thomas Challis was serving time despite a determined trawl of calendars of indictments and minutes of evidence. That left only one option, contemporary newspaper reports. The Old Bailey sessions papers brought nothing and the digital archives also had no lead so the search switched to local newspapers and ultimate reward for the diligence. I was able to report back on his misdemeanours.

Under the Public Records Acts of 1958 and 1967, those records 'of historical and public interest' are kept for 30 years before being transferred from prisons to local archive collections. The Prison Service Order first issued in 1995 and again in 1999 has this directive; 'Destruction of Old Records: There is no need to keep records more than 30 years old which are of no historical interest and which are not in administrative use. Your archivist will indicate which records are of value, and you can destroy the rest.'

Historians cringe at the statement, one person's idea of

what constitutes public interest is another's journal of historic record. The rules are clear regarding the period of time that must elapse before a member of the public can see prison records: execution records and registers of officers: 40 years after last use. Governors' journals, chaplains' journals, medical officers' journals, visiting committee rota and minute books and condemned cell occurrence books: 70 years after last use. Prisoners' calendars with identification of victims: 100 years after last use. The Prison Service Order was a sensible attempt to streamline record preservation however, the needs of family historians were hardly a priority at the time so persistence is essential. Fortunately for researchers, most convicts have re-offended and their names will appear elsewhere. I once investigated an offender whose crime was committed in Manchester and found his name eventually in Dartmoor. Plus, it is not uncommon for prisoners to become 'invisible' mostly by changing their name on release.

One particular Yorkshire prisoner I was searching for, a Sheffield agitator back in the time of the Chartists, when men were campaigning – often too violently – for suffrage legislation to change, I eventually found record of in a provincial jail, because he wasn't initially recognised as a 'political' prisoner.

What has become known as the Sheffield Plot of 1840 involved Samuel Holberry, William Martin – the man I was tracing, Thomas Booker and others devising an attempted coup in the city in which they planned to seize the Town Hall and the Fortune Inn, set fire to the magistrate's court, and then, linking with other Chartists, join together insurrections in Nottingham and Rotherham. Their plot was betrayed by James Allen and Lord Howard the Lord Lieutenant, took immediate action. The result was that, at York Assizes on 22nd March 1840, Holberry was sentenced to four years at

Northallerton for seditious conspiracy: 'And at the expiration of that period to be bound himself in £50 and to find two sureties in ten shillings each, to keep the peace towards his Majesty's subjects.'

He was leniently treated; under an Act of 1351 he could have had life imprisonment. The Chartists wanted electoral reform and votes for working men, along with a boundary change of electoral districts. In the years around 1840, the 'Physical Force' arm of that movement was accelerating and the Sheffield men were out to take extreme measures. William Martin was given a sentence of one year at Northallerton and he became such a problem that the issue reached parliament. His charge was seditious language and his behaviour in court tells us a great deal about the man. The *Times* reported, 'On sentence being passed, he struck his hand on the front of the dock, saying: 'Well that will produce a revolution, if anything will.' He begged his Lordship not to send him to Northallerton but to let him remain in the castle at York, saying that he was very comfortable, and having been seven months confined already was quite at home.'

To Northallerton Martin went and there he was to stir things up. In court he had already stressed his Irish connections and made reference to Irish issues. 'He entered into 'a long harangue' on Orangemen, the King of Hanover and Rathcormac' the report included. Martin refused to work on the treadmill as he had not been sentenced to hard labour. He was put into the refractory cell for that refusal, but his case was supported by the Secretary of State, Lord Normanby, who wrote: '...the prisoner, who was not sentenced to hard labour, cannot legally be placed upon the wheel against his consent... and that if he should refuse to labour upon the wheel, it would be illegal for the gaoler to place him in solitary confinement.'

But a visiting magistrate argued against this by quoting one of Peel's recent Gaol Acts which allowed for the work done on a treadmill to be defined as either hard labour or as, ' employment for those who are required by law to work for their maintenance...' Martin, as far as we know, was compelled to work on the mill and he subsequently claimed savage treatment at the hands of the Northallerton staff. He is recorded as saying: 'One morning as soon as I had left my cell, the Governor's son... took me by the collar and dragged me from the place where I stood and threw me with violence against the wall, and on the following day he told me I must expect different treatment from what I received in York and he added that men had been reduced to mere skeletons when their term of imprisonment expired and that it should be the case with me...'

The Governor's son, William Shepherd, was indeed a character. Even in his teens he was the scourge of the felons. Quiet was enforced by a so-called 'keeper of silence' and in 1837 Shepherd, as the young man holding that position, the son of the Keeper and the Matron, wrote to his friend in York. His letter gives us a clear picture of the problems in maintaining vigilance and control.

It read, 'Dear George, I have received your letter. Your apprenticeship with your uncle in York is no doubt of great interest. You seem displeased with your lot against mine. To answer you, yes, my father is Keeper of the prison and mother is the Matron. They did give me the post at £50 a year, but George, this is a House of Correction, and Inspectors visit regularly. One has just made his visit and he said I was very youthful for such a position [he was aged 17] which requires great moderation and command of temper. He also added and put down in his report, during the course of his inspection he had no reason to believe the post to be inadequately filled. The parson caused quite a to do just before the Inspector arrived. He likes to distribute tracts and books to the untried prisoners. The Inspector looked through them and found a piece on secret writing and invisible ink. When he visited our hospital he found some of our prisoners experimenting with it... It's not easy this job, George, the prisoners are wily as foxes. If any infringe the rules, I take them before the Keeper. I took one boy yesterday for turning his head to the side while reading. He answered he was obliged to do so as it was so dark in the mess room. Father believed him and let him go unpunished. He said it was no offence. I wasn't best pleased, I'm sure he was preparing to whisper to a friend. Next time, I'll wait until he does so, then I'll have him in solitary. He won't dupe me.' William was governor by 1849, succeeding his father, Thomas.

Northallerton, now derelict, was a very old prison estate going back in the form of a bridewell or house of correction, to the late eighteenth century. In the years following the end of the Great War in 1918, several prisons were closed and in 1922 Northallerton ceased operations, though the buildings were left standing. When global war came along in 1939 the site was in use again, this time as a training depot for the military police. The cells provided accommodation for the trainees, and it was transformed into a busy military location, principally centred around the prevention of sabotage. In 1943 it was needed as a prison once again and became a military detention centre. By 1946, Northallerton was national news, as the location of an uprising that became known as 'The Glass-House Mutiny.'

In the House of Commons on 26th March, 1946, Secretary of State Jack Lawson responded to Tom Driberg with regard to an enquiry into conditions at Stakehill Detention Centre, near Bolton. Reported in *The Times*,

'[Lawson] said that he had recently received the final report of the Court of Inquiry into conditions at Stakehill detention barracks. The general conclusion was that the allegations which had been made in the public press and in letters to the Rev. Urien Evans, or to members of Parliament, were either unfounded or grossly exaggerated. The Court of Inquiry, which included among the members a KC and a psychiatrist, examined every aspect of the problem in great detail. Every effort was made to call as witnesses all those who had made allegations about the treatment of prisoners at Stakehill, and also all soldiers under sentence who had any complaint to make. They examined in all 195 witnesses including 47 members or ex-members of staff...'

It all appeared very thorough, but his conclusion, 'That there is no need to make any further enquiry into conditions at Stakehill' is very much at odds with personal testimony and similar prison conditions affected Northallerton severely.

Albert Meltzer, who had also been detained in Brixton wrote that he found the North Yorkshire establishment, 'seething with mutiny.' He saw that something was deeply wrong, and he noted that many of those being abused were 'a credit to the nation.' He pointed out that the cruelty was often extreme: 'Yet for some minor infraction of absurdly imposed regulations or breach of discipline... we were kept in cages.'

There were similar scenes at Aldershot, where the disturbances involved several soldiers recently transferred from Northallerton, which then became the subject of the next bout of insurrection. On 1st March rioters there forced their way into one of the prison stores and set fire to it. Some of the men climbed onto the roof and began throwing bricks. The local fire brigade arrived and put out the fire. The rioting took place in a hall holding 70 men. They were long-sentence prisoners and matters quickly became a condition of extreme danger: armed soldiers from Catterick camp were called in and a cordon was placed around the block. Officers and managers acted quickly and efficiently to ensure that the rioters could not get near the armoury.

The leading lights in the insurrection were from the British Army of the Rhine and the main source a unit that had served in Italy, with the disaffection that began there carried with them back to England, not least that sentences for quite minor offences were deemed very long. The *Daily Mail* photographer managed to take a flight over the prison and get shots showing all the events and of the destruction. Their main headline said: 'National Glasshouse Plot Suspected.' It was a case of hype on a grand scale. 'Seven long-term prisoners, bedraggled and shivering – they had been drenched by hose-water for hours – climbed down from the rafters of this military prison at 7.45 tonight after a roof-top siege which lasted eight and a half hours. So ended an all-day riot involving nearly 300 soldiers.' Reporter Reginald Butler went on to say that, 'Most of Northallerton's century-old prison was wrecked' – which was clearly grossly inaccurate.

There was a trial of the mutineers. The men had originally gone AWOL after serving well in the theatre of war and their sense of injustice is not difficult to imagine.

On 27th April, it was reported that 11 of the soldiers were charged with mutiny and faced court-martials at Catterick camp. They were from the Pioneer Corps, The Royal Scots, The Royal Northumberland Fusiliers, the General Service Corps, The Seaforth Highlanders, and (most ironically) from The Loyal Regiment. The men were named and shamed in the national press. In 2016, Northallerton prison was finally closed. The likelihood is that the one part of it that survives will be the Governor's house, which was designed and built by one of Yorkshire's most famous architects, John Carr.

Researching Yorkshire's prisons has also brought out some fascinating footnotes in criminal history. For instance, it was at Hull that a milestone in policing history was achieved. The first police dog section ever created was at Hull docks in 1908. The dogs were named Jim, Vic, Mick and Ben, and they stole the limelight in the national press from their handler, Sergeant Allison. The *Penny Pictorial* magazine wrote: 'In a novel experiment by the North Eastern Railway Police, dogs are being used as detectives on the docks at Hull. They consist of a number of trained Airedale terriers which patrol throughout the day and night...'

In 1910, the terriers made a significant arrest, as the railway police magazine reported. 'Early one morning a policeman accompanied by a dog was patrolling St Andrews Dock and, seeing a man loitering in a suspicious manner called upon him to stop. The man took no notice and the policeman slipped his dog – one of the best. The dog soon had the man trapped.' The window of a refreshment room was found broken, two other men inside. Three burly fellows were escorted to the police station and they were soon in Hull prison, it turning out that they were notorious burglars within the city. A new dog training centre was opened at Hedon Hall after the First World War run by Inspector John Morrell, who started breeding dogs for special uses.

Hull was also the scene of one of the most dramatic and controversial executions in British criminal history. All eyes across the nation were on HMP Hull when Ethel Major was waiting to die there just before Christmas, 1934. From Kirkby-on-Bain, Lincolnshire, the 43-year-old was convicted for the murder of her husband, Arthur, the previous May by use of strychnine. Another to give no evidence in her defence, she was sent to Hull for the execution to avoid the almost certain public disturbances which would have happened had she been hanged in Lincoln. Alderman Stark of Hull wrote a last appeal for clemency, saying, 'For the sake of humanity I implore you to reconsider your decision, especially having regard to the nearness of Christmas... The heartfelt pleas contained in this telegram are those of 30,000 inhabitants and particularly those of the women of this great city.'

The sense of defeat and the inevitable conclusion on the scaffold was hovering over her defence from the beginning. Lord Birkett's memoirs contain his view that Crown Counsel had opened with a statement that had a ring of finality: 'The case is really on the evidence unanswerable.' One of the very best defence lawyers in the land could do nothing. It seems odd with this in mind that the *Daily Express* had insisted that, 'Nobody believes she will be hanged', just a few weeks before the sentence. There was no way that an appeal based on the unfairness of the judge's summing up would succeed.

At her hanging, young Albert Pierrepoint accompanied his uncle Henry. As Steve Fielding has recorded, in his biography of the Pierrepoints: 'When they returned to their quarters, Albert asked his uncle a question. 'What are women like? What do you have to do – anything special?' Smiling slowly, his uncle answered, 'Why lad, you're not afraid are you?' 'No,' he replied, 'I was just wondering.' Tom put his hand on his nephew's shoulder and reassured him there was nothing to worry about: 'I shall be very surprised if Mrs Major isn't calmer than any man you have seen so far...'

Ethel Major did go firmly and courageously to her date with the noose. I have been to that prison and seen the death cell and the 'execution suite' as it was termed. I did the walk and counted the time, going from the small condemned cell to the spot where she would have been placed ready for the drop. It took 20 seconds. Looking back at the case today, one feels a sense of outrage, not only at the harsh treatment of the woman and the unfeeling process of law, but also at the persistence of that well-entrenched belief that when a woman – the 'fairer sex' – kills, it is so extremely against 'nature' that the letter of the law should erase a full understanding of the emotional and individual circumstances.

As staff at Hull are only too aware, that is not the end of the Major story. Reputedly her presence walks the landings, several officers have reported seeing 'the ghost of the lady.' Mrs Major has entered the folklore as well as the history of HMP Hull.

7

•

THE STRANGE WORLD
OF THE CRIMINAL COURTS

Hunting for stories and truth in the criminal annals of Yorkshire, it soon becomes apparent that the focus for the most powerful and compelling tales is the courtroom. Since 1971 we have had the Crown Courts for serious cases along with the higher courts, but across the centuries, the famous and infamous have stood in the dock at the assizes.

The story of the assize courts is a reflection of how criminal law gradually developed and found a system which would have parity across the land.

Those courts represent the boldest step by which central legal power began to cover the King's domains, holding the local and the national elements together. In each shire, the sheriff, who had been there since very early times, gathered the jury and the other machinery of law, ready for the visit of the assize judges – courts done in transit – giving the toured towns distinguished visitors and a high level of ritual and importance for a few days each year.

Since early Medieval times, there had been assizes – 'sittings together' – to try causes and to gather officials in the English regions to compile enquiries and inventories into local possessions and actions. These were 'eyres' of assize, but they were not courts. The assize courts came when travelling justices went out into the shires to hear cases, these became known as circuits. What developed over the centuries was that serious offences, crimes needing an indictment, had to go before a jury.

The less serious offences, summary ones, could be tried by a magistrate. In addition to that, the terms felony and misdemeanour also existed until they were abolished in 1967: a felony was a crime in which guilt would mean a forfeiture of possessions and land, so the offender's children would lose their inheritance. A misdemeanour was a less serious offence.

The justices of assize had a number of powers.

First, they had a commission of oyer and terminer (to listen and to act) on serious cases such as treason, murder and any crime which was labelled a felony. They also had to try all people who had been charged and languishing in gaol since their arrest. The assize circuits became established as the Home, Midland, Norfolk, Oxford, Eastern, Western and Northern, and ran from 1558 to either 1864 or 1876 when assizes were reorganised, or to 1971, when they were abolished and crown courts created. From the beginning, the assize circuits covered all counties except Cheshire, Durham, Lancashire and Middlesex.

The result of all this means that a criminal ancestor who committed a crime in Leeds, for instance, after 1876, would be tried in Leeds rather than in York, the former seat for the West Riding.

The family historian needs to access the location of the court and trial as a first step. A useful source for checking on which assizes were on the circuit at any time between the late eighteenth century and the end of the nineteenth is *The Gentleman's Magazine*, which listed them and names of judges presiding at each one. This journal appeared annually. The assizes were held twice a year from the thirteenth century and these sessions were referred to as Spring and Winter. A third session could be held at times if the gaols were full – as in times of popular revolt and riots, or activities by gangs.

The assizes were divided into two areas: for civil cases, referred to as 'crown' – and criminal cases. Two judges would be on the road, each with a responsibility for one of the areas. Newspapers tend to use the terms, 'crown side' and 'criminal side.'

The York and Leeds assizes were where the nefarious rogues such as Turpin, Peace and Aram stood to be judged and sentenced, but alongside these high profile cases, we have the everyday courts run by the magistrates until the nineteenth century when they were often referred to as the police courts.

Of the courts run by the bench of magistrates, the quarter sessions were the ones that saw their fair share of crime, in all its variety. Those courts were the workhorse of the criminal justice system throughout British history.

They began in 1351 and handled every kind of offence and local tribulation. They were the domain of the justices of the peace and met, as the name suggests, four times a year. In front of them came concerns relating to drunkenness, pub brawls, arguments over land, nuisances on the highway, problems with beggars, licensing of beer houses, provision of constables, maintenance of bridges and other affairs; the topics changing as the years passed and society had new laws and fresh social problems. All the justices of the county generally sat on the bench at quarter sessions.

Matters were running smoothly through the years until an Act of 1831 which stipulated specific dates for the courts, so as not to interfere with the assizes. It said, 'Quarter sessions for the peace by law ought to be held… in the first week after the 11th of October, in the first week after the 28th of December, in the first week after the 31st of March, and in the first week after the 24th of June.' From the early nineteenth century, details of the sessions were given in almanacs, sometimes locally but always in the *British Almanac*, published by the Society for the Diffusion of Useful Knowledge. This publication listed all the quarter sessions for the coming year, with dates and venues.

It was in the Tudor period that the justices really found their workload accelerating as a succession of legislative measures to deal with the increasing problems of vagrants, wanderers from other parishes and disabled soldiers, and also of affairs relating to apprentices and workmen, street crime and the regulation of all local matters pertaining to the social order were issued.

The magistrates were first created as a fresh form of the previous 'Keeper of the Peace' and it is no accident that they appeared, and were more clearly defined, at a time of massive social crisis. The Black Death of 1348 and the horrendous years of famine previous to that, along with other epidemics and social revolt, made the year 1361 one of the most significant in British legal history. It was followed by an Act which set up quarter sessions the next year. The immediate context was one of the widespread threat of violence and roving gangs across the land.

Quarter sessions dealt with capital offences until the 1660s and from that time there were also an increasing number of petty sessions, hearings often dealing with many of the matters the more prominent court normally handled. The everyday offences before the magistrates were misdemeanours, crimes that could be tried without a jury. In the nineteenth century, many local offences were dealt with by police courts, which were yet another form of petty session, but the quarter sessions continued, the centre of the great law machine in the heart of the social upheavals of the Industrial Revolution, when massive threats of riot and disorder were everywhere including the Luddites 'Captain Swing' rural crime and the rise of the Chartist movement which added to the burden of the justices.

In his book, *A Farmer's Year* (1899) we have accounts of novelist H. Rider Haggard's work as a justice in Norfolk where he was an important landowner, and he reflects on some petty crimes from June 1898, hearing a case of egg-stealing, in which a man described as a marine dealer was accused of sending a box of 251 partridge eggs to another dealer. He was fined a shilling an egg or two months in gaol. Haggard's thoughts on poaching give us an insight into some of the main issues magistrates dealt with. He notes, '...I have on several occasions seen poaching cases dismissed when the evidence would have been thought sufficient to ensure conviction... it is extraordinary what an amount of false sentiment is wasted in certain quarters upon poachers, who, for the most part, are very cowardly villains...' It was rife in the sweeping Wolds and Dales of Yorkshire.

In his note for 20th April in the same year, there is a case of lunacy. He writes, in his capacity as the magistrate appointed to be in action in cases under the Lunacy Acts. 'About breakfast time on Sunday morning I was requested by an overseer to attend in a neighbouring village to satisfy myself by personal examination as to the madness of a certain pauper lunatic...' He did indeed agree and signed the orders needed for her removal to an asylum. It was a sad occasion and a huge responsibility. He adds, 'It seems that it was not considered advisable that the patient should remain longer out of proper control, so, as she could not be removed without a magistrate's order, I was followed to the church.' The justices had a massive amount of responsibility before them and had to deal with several issues related to non-judicial duties as well as the criminal cases needing due process of law.

There was generally a sequence of actions and topics in how trials at quarter sessions were conducted. First there would be presentments applied to all the waiting accused, statements of the alleged offences. Typically; John Holmes of Keighley, blacksmith, for assaulting there on 13th March and maltreating John Greene, clerk. Witn. Ja. Ibbetson... (Puts himself not guilty at Skipton 18t July 1638).' Then there would be Appeals and Supervisions, These could include assessments of property, highway maintenance fines, repairs of bridges, issues relating to parish constables, financial accounts of various people in office, appeals against assessments and, until the Municipal Corporations Act of 1835, supervising boards of health, poor law unions and town councils. The non-judicial duties retained after that were mainly of licensing premises, arbitrating in master and servant disputes, supervising county rates, the sale of coals, bread and flour regulations and ensuring that friendly societies and trade unions.

Finally, there were Orders – all matters of a parish or civil nature. They were most clearly seen at times of peril and threat towards the authorities, for instance during the Luddite violence around 1811-1812 or the Chartists agitations of the 1830s and 1840s. Equally, in the Tudor period and through to the 1834 Poor Law reforms, there would be issues such as vagrancy and social responsibility. The 1637 sessions for the West Riding record a long list of crimes, most were felonies and one possible punishment was death. Reading the account today, there is a deep sense of foreboding in the wording. For example, 16 men and two women were, 'Put for good or ill upon the country, whereupon a jury was called... they were led to the bar by the sheriff and asked what they could say for themselves why they should not have judgement of death according to the law for the felonies aforesaid whereof they were convicted. They severally said that they were clerks and prayed for benefit of clergy to be granted them.'

The 'Benefit of Clergy' ruling meant that if a felon could read what was called the 'neck verse' – which they could claim on only one occasion - then they would be branded rather than hanged. It was the opening of the 51st psalm. 'Have mercy upon me, O God, according to Thy loving kindness: according to the multitude of Thy tender mercies blot out my transgressions.' The neck verse was originally intended to give clergy an exemption from the criminal law process. An old poem of the period explains:

> 'If a clerk had been taken
> For stealing of bacon,
> For burglary, murder or rape.
> If he could but rehearse
> (well prompt) his neck verse,
> He never could fail to escape.'

But the unhappy line of men and women in 1637, although they had learned the words well, had further pain to come. By virtue of Henry VII they had to be branded, each burned on their left hand, according to a statute which said, 'Every person so convicted of murder, be marked with an M upon the brawn of the left thumb, and if he be convicted for any other felony the same person to be marked with a T in the same place upon the thumb, and these marks to be made by a gaoler openly in court before the judge.'

Such courtroom trials provide the strangest tales. They were, effectively, petty kingdoms, run by magistrates or, at assizes, by the King's justices who arrived in a grand parade, were regally entertained and fed and then let loose in their domain to meter out punishment.

Coming to Yorkshire, those who presided in either kind of court were in for some bizarre experiences, as in this case of a man who never replied to any question. 'York Assizes: Abraham Bairstan, aged 60, was put to the bar, charged with the wilful murder of Sarah Bairstan his wife, in the parish of Bradford.'

The case from 1824 gives us an insight into the plight of those unfortunates at the time who were victims of ignorance as well as of illness. In this instance it was an awful, anguished mental illness that played a major part in the murder. When the turnkey brought Bairstan into the court he commented that he had not heard the prisoner say a word since he was brought to York and locked up.

This was nothing new to the man's family. Mr. Baron Hullock, presiding, was shocked but also full of that natural curiosity of someone who just does not understand something. He pressed the gaoler to explain. He asked if the man in the dock understood the spoken word and the answer was no. He also ascertained that Bairstan appeared to have no response to any sound whatsoever, nor any movement. It makes painful reading in the court report to note that the prisoner was a, 'Dull and heavy looking man who... cast a vacant glance around the court.' The reporter present noted that the man, 'Appeared totally insensible of the nature of the proceedings.'

Hullock had a real challenge to try to communicate with the man, trying his best to make the prisoner make any sound at all, asking several questions but receiving no answer. When he asked 'Do you hear what I say to you?' Bairstan simply stared at the officer next to him. It was apparently going to be one of those trials at which many people were thinking that this silence was the best ruse if a man wanted to avoid the rope. The judge had to instruct the jury about this being a potential act and the possibility that they were faced with an amoral killer with a canny wit and impressive acting skills, standing there fraudulently, wilfully and obstinately.

Enter his sons and a close friend, Jeremiah Hailey, who told a very sad and astounding story. His friend stated that he had known the prisoner for over 50 years and that he was sure that ten years had passed since Bairstan had fallen silent. He explained that his two sons had been looking after the old man during that time. His key statement was that: 'While he was sane, his wife and he had lived together very comfortably.' Hailey added that his friend had since been capable of merely saying yes or no, and that the last time he had heard the man speak was when he had asked him if he knew his friend.

'He said aye, but I think he did not know me.'

Bairstan's two sons confirmed that their father had been silent in that ten-year period, only excepting one or two words. Henry said that since being locked up, his father had been pressed to speak and had answered something sounding like. 'Be quiet... be quiet'. The other son, Joseph, confirmed that his father had been: 'Out of his mind for ten years.' There had been enough in him to marry and earn a living, but we must see with hindsight and more relevant knowledge, that Abraham Bairstan had been struck by a paralysis, perhaps combined with a depressive mental illness. In 1824, the most meaningful explanation was to put it down to God's will, so the jury found that the prisoner stood mute, 'By the visitation of God' and guilty of the crime.

Sometimes at the magistrates' courts, before any professional police or detectives were formed, the man in charge took it upon himself to play sleuth. The popular history books and press of the time have given us a general picture of the eighteenth century magistrate that tends to suggest an idle, over-fed and peremptory fellow, too keen to have the next meal and put felons inside to cool off. Perhaps this owes a lot to the novels of the time. But documents do indicate that a typical magistrate need not have stirred from a comfortable chair unless there was an extreme emergency.

There was, at least, one exception in the Bradford and Halifax area between 1751 and 1769. Samuel Lister was a formidable man to have as an enemy. Unluckily for those involved in the 'yellow trade' of coining and clipping at this time and in the risky act of forgery, he was more than capable of going out and playing investigator when needed. Lister was based at Horton House, and he had been trained as an attorney and spent 13 years in practice. He had to stop that when he took up the magistrate's post.

His father had served on the bench for the West Riding, and the area covering Bradford and Calderdale was vast, mostly wild and empty, and in the first stages of an industrial revolution, meaning Lister was kept considerably busy. At that time there were around two hundred capital offences and also plenty of lock-ups, stocks and houses of correction to keep the less serious offenders out of circulation for a while. In 1764, in the Halifax parish of his area, there was a population of approximately 40,000, and no magistrate in local residence when Lister stepped into the role. Bradford at the time had three justices but he was a remarkable man, highly regarded by the Marquis of Rockingham, the outstanding legal figure for the West Riding based at York Castle.

Lister had plenty to occupy him in the activities of thieves and robbers and averaged about 26 sittings each year. One delinquent he set his sights on was William Wilkins, a known forger. He had been arrested and brought to the court for not paying bills at various hostelries throughout the region. He had been searched and interrogated and on his person were found letters, one with a Gloucester postmark and, more astonishingly, a promissory note for the huge sum of £1,100 – a massive fortune at that time. They were clearly forgeries and, if proven, he would be liable to be hanged. Wilkins claimed he was from Painswick in Somerset and trying to communicate with the relevant authorities there was something usually far too strenuous and time-consuming for your average magistrate to bother with. Not Samuel Lister, though, he was a determined man with a sense of challenge.

The first step was to enlist some qualified assistance, so he turned to the Leeds Recorder, Richard Wilson. The two men decided to keep Wilkins locked up while information was gathered, putting items in London newspapers and sending messages to Gloucester. They were pushed for time. Wilkins was also due to appear at the Lent Assizes in the South West and likely had friends or business acquaintances there to stand bail for him. Because if his network of contacts, Lister's use of the 'grapevine' around Bradford paid off, and one contact knew of a West Country man currently visiting, a Walter Merrett. Merritt told Lister to write to a clothier at

Uley near Painswick, to ascertain the necessary information and identification. It was a triumph. 'Wilkins' turned out to be Edward Wilson from Painswick, wanted for forgery. The felon was sent to trial at Gloucester on 20th March, 1756 and was sentenced to death.

Lister also got to work against the clippers. This yellow trade involved filing or clipping coins down to an acceptable weight for local use and thereby creating more coins with the clippings; it was very lucrative, and a capital offence ranked as high treason. The risks were high and it made the criminals act with desperation and resolve, even to the extent of murder, as in the case of the excise man William Deighton, killed in Halifax in 1769. It was no easy task to attempt to find and prosecute the perpetrators, though, the trade enjoyed considerable popular support. Lister again made it his crusade to. Still the best way to find out the villains was to employ agents provocateurs and Lister, together with John Hustler in Bradford, did that successfully, their work leading to the arrest of two men on an inspector's evidence who were packed off to York Castle.

Samuel Lister saw the magistracy not only as something opening up opportunities to act on behalf of the law itself and civil order, but as a means of reinforcing authority in an economic context also, partly because he had links with local industrialists, protecting the value and nexus of coins in trade circulation. His principal biographer, John Styles, quotes Lister's own words as explanation of his motives. 'I think it my duty not only as a magistrate but as a private person to do all that I am able to bring villains to justice.'

There was similar high drama in the assizes, where more organized crime was tried, not least that of highwaymen. I was researching a certain Spence Broughton of York and was told at the museum that there was an interesting holding warehouse in an industrial estate, to the edge of the city that might offer further clues. There were indeed some interesting pieces there, including a splinter of thick wood with a flap of cloth attached. 'This is from the gibbet of a highwayman,' I was informed. 'In fact, there's a jug as well... maybe a tea set... made from his bones!'

Broughton was a man who could have been a successful farmer, had he stayed on the right side of the law. He had a farm bought for him at Marton, near Sleaford, when he was just 22. He also gathered more wealth when he married a woman who brought money with her as a dowry but even that was not enough for him. He began by gambling and mixed with bad company, including a certain John Oxley.

With Oxley, contact started with a London fence called Shaw and soon Broughton and his friend were taking on robberies. They were paid to intercept the Rotherham mail. Setting out from Chesterfield, not far from the town on the Dearne, the two men stopped the coach which only had a post-boy driving who was tied up and left. The robbers took the mail bag but there was little worth having in it, except a bill of exchange for a large sum. While Broughton stayed in Mansfield, Oxley went to London with it. His problem was to convert it into money but in the capital, with the help of Shaw who had set up the job they managed to, using a company in Austin Friars. After giving Broughton just £10 initially, Oxley found himself at the point of being pressured for more and it seems that Broughton raised his share to five times that.

Having come across a simple means of stealing funds, they were soon out on the road again, robbing the Cambridge mail this time, and their difficulties began because a provincial bank note was traced, one of a number that the two men had been working hard to spend. Thanks to the energetic and sharp-eyed work of a shop boy, Bow Street officers found the lodgings where Broughton was staying and, after a chase, cornered him at an inn called The Dog and Duck. Broughton was taken to Bow Street, Shaw turned King's evidence and told the whole story of the robbery at Cambridge and where and how they had dealt with and hidden the takings. Later, the two men were cross-examined again, and although the post-boy could not identify them, they were remanded in custody. The enterprising and wily Oxley managed to escape from Clerkenwell bridewell, disappearing into the night and we know nothing more of him. But Broughton was taken north to York. He was tried before Mr Justice Buller at the Spring Assizes in 1792. Shaw again testified against him and also a man called Close who had assisted in the financial transactions in London. Broughton was told by the judge that there was, 'Not a shadow of hope' of any mercy.

Spence Broughton was sentenced to be hanged and also gibbeted. He was reported as having faced that sentence with fortitude and he prepared himself for death. He perished with four others on 14th April, 1792, and before he died said: 'This is the happiest day that I have experienced for some time.' The story does not end there, however. His body was gibbeted on Attercliffe Common, not far from the Arrow Inn and there was a local feast day, with his body being pulleyed up into position on the Monday morning. Some years later, when some of the bones of the highwayman had loosened and fallen, the tale is told of a local potter who took the skeleton's fingers and used them to make some bone china items. One of these, a jug, was sold in London in 1871. Such is the notoriety of this Sheffield rogue that over the years, people have hoarded and preserved anything related to his story and in one of the York archive stores, that piece of the gibbet is still preserved.

Another hold-up man famous in folk memory, was the one who performed 'Nevison's Ride' – a feat wrongly attributed to Dick Turpin, who attained mythical status as a gentleman of the road although in truth was a rapist, killer and horse-stealer. In 1699, a newspaper report gave the following details of a robbery. 'Last week, in the dusk of the evening, three highwaymen set upon a country farm... the farmer and his friend got two of the highwaymen down, but the third coming up, shot the farmer through and killed him...' William Nevison was that killer, a man most likely born in Wortley near Pontefract and hanged in York in 1684. Most areas in Yorkshire like to claim him as their own, notably in the burgeoning heritage industry, but what is not widely known is that there is a strong oral tradition that he was active around Gomersal and Hartshead, and his most well recounted deed there was also a murder when he shot the landlord of a public house near Batley.

Nevison's infamy across the West Riding and also the South Yorkshire stretch of the Great North Road made him the subject of ballads and apocryphal tales; there is a cutting at Castleford called Nevison's leap and an inn was given his name. The song 'Bold Nevison' has some patently untrue statements:

> 'I have never robbed no man of tuppence
> and I've never done murder nor killed.
> Though guilty I've been all my lifetime,
> So gentlemen do as you please.'

The story most associated with him and the feat that won him the nickname 'Swift Nick' was a ride north to his native county after a robbery at Gads Hill in Kent in 1676, making his escape on a bay mare, riding north at an incredibly fast pace, some say going from Kent to York in a day.

We know that his father was a steward at Wortley Hall and his brother was a schoolmaster, and that Nevison married and had a daughter. Incredibly, his wife lived on to be 109-years-old. The oral tales pass on a complimentary view of Nevison, that he was tall, charming and never used violence. The truth seems to be very different.

A diary entry for 1727 recalls a memory of Nevison, saying he was living with the Skelton family – gamekeepers at Wortley. It reads, 'At the same time there lived with this Skelton Nevison, who afterwards was an excise man, but being out of his place, became a highwayman.' He effectively became gamekeeper turned poacher, crossing to the wrong side of the law. Further investigation reveals that he began his criminal career early, stealing when he was only 14. James Sharpe, in his book about Dick Turpin, says, 'After being punished for stealing a silver spoon from his father, he (Nevison) stole ten pounds from his father and his horse, set off for London, cutting his horse and slitting its throat outside the capital in case he be suspected...'

It is hard to believe that the robber who haunted the Leeds to Manchester Road around what is now Hartshead and the northern fringe of Mirfield was also once in service with the Duke of York at the siege of Dunkirk. Everything about him fits the description given him in the Victorian period when the myths were fully generated of him as 'The Northern Claude Duval', Duval was the most famous of the gentlemanly highwaymen and the man whose life was once spared by Royal clemency.

Nevison's capture is as uncertain and undefined as his life. He used to visit one of his girls at Royd Nook and would call in an old inn called The King's Head, north of Mirfield. He would most likely make his way from that base onto the roadside and wait for the Manchester coach. It would be a good corridor to 'work', along what is now close to the M62. But the tale is told of him stopping at an inn in Batley while on these excursions, just to take a drink and the landlord recognised him. The man raised the alarm but Nevison was quick, and as the landlord came to tackle him just as the robber was mounting his horse, he was shot and killed. Nevison was found, taken to York and hanged.

He always had a reputation that placed him in the Robin Hood tradition, mainly due to Lord Macaulay's famous *History of England*, in which the renowned historian says that, 'The great robber of the north of Yorkshire levied a quarterly tribute on all northern drovers, and in return not only spared them himself but protected them against all other thieves; that he demanded purses in the most courteous manner, and that he gave largely to the poor...'

Through the centuries, up until mid-Victorian times, there was a scourge that threatened everyone in the courts – whether the alleged perpetrator in the dock, the spectators in the public gallery or the legal professionals. That was gaol fever, or typhus. The prisoners contracted it in their cells while waiting for months for the assize judges to arrive on the circuit. It is easy to see why so many prisoners died in the prisons in the Georgian days. The local cell at Knaresborough, for instance, was under the hall and had an earth floor, it was running with rats and two sewers flowed through it. When the prison reformer, John Howard, inspected it, he was told that the turnkey often took his dog with him to fight off the rats but, on one occasion, the rats killed the dog and attacked the man in the face.

At one court in Oxford in 1577, everyone who had been

present at a trial died within 48 hours of the case being concluded.

Occasionally, some people survived long stretches in prison and one Leeds man, John Dufreni, surely holds a record here. After refusing to answer questions from a commission on bankruptcy he was locked up for 43 years and died in the infirmary. There has always been a tendency in British prisons for some inmates to be completely forgotten.

8

•

INSIDE THE CRIMINAL MIND

Whether I am writing true crime or crime fiction, there is a common element involved, what might best be called negative empathy.

In reading about either the high tragedy of a villain who kills his wife through crazed jealousy, or in enjoying a crafted story in a popular magazine, the protagonist does things that ask for some kind of reasoning. The reader applies empathy in trying to understand incomprehensible actions, some kind of mitigating circumstances.

Today, we have greater feel for psychology but in earlier times, not so. Crime stories tended to involve a long fall from power and status. The concept partly explains why there are people who marry Death Row inmates and other lifers, and a crime writer needs an element of this negative empathy somewhere in the planning and writing of the tale.

Murder in Mind

In Jewish literature and tradition, the nebbish character has been developed by modern novelists, and screen writers such as Woody Allen and Larry David – a man whose weakness and hubris is as powerful as anything in classical tragedy. The crimes don't have to be horrible murder, simply a moral lapse than crosses the line into some kind of offence. Equally, it may be a crime borne of some kind of mental illness, exemplified by Hitchcock's *Psycho*.

Looking for local source material, I was told this by a home help. 'I used to go to this frail couple. You'd have thought a strong breeze would have flattened them. They were very old. She was thin as a brush, with matted grey hair and skin trouble. She was very ill, poor lass. A chilling little girl's voice would come out of the bedclothes, when I thought she'd snoozed off. 'I've cleaned the cellar mummy!' the voice would say, in a sort of whimpering tone. He was broody, often somewhere else, dreaming or occupying himself with daft jobs. He was always a shadow in the background. You'd be washing up or sweeping the steps, and you'd just be aware of him, out of the corner of your eye. The woman was bed-ridden, I had to turn her a lot. The place stank to high heaven. By God I did some washing. I tried everything to rid the place of that smell. The whole place was awful – and I've seen some grim places. This old love, she used to tell me her dreams all the time. But one particular dream she kept having terrified her. It was about an old lady with long grey hair who came to see her in the night. It started with a shadow on the lace curtain by the kitchen door, then a gentle voice said: 'For you, dearest.' Then she'd be hit in the face and about the chest and shoulders. I started to hate going there. One day, making the bed, I came across this grey wig, stuffed down behind the end of the bed-head. He'd been wearing it and attacking her and he always seemed so harmless.'

The perpetrator never appeared in court, it was just another example of a Yorkshire domestic incident committed within the family.

A more notorious case was published as a popular pamphlet in 1605 as *The Yorkshire Tragedy*. In 1608 it became a play and was printed as being written by William Shakespeare. Scholarship since then has shown that it was almost certainly not. The story is based on events at Calverley Hall, near Bradford, and an horrendous and bloody murder by a father of his sons. He also stabbed his poor wife.

Walter Calverley had married Philippa Brooke in 1599, the aunt of Sir Robert Cecil, the first earl of Salisbury, who as Queen Elizabeth I's chief minister, skillfully directed the government during the first nine years of the reign of King James and gave continuity to the change from Tudor to Stuart rule. What actually happened that awful day in April 1605 we will almost certainly never know in detail. Calverley had severe mounting debts. He had been selling off much of his extensive land in the East Riding as well as property around his home in Pudsey, Burley and Menston. The couple had only been married for a year when he was imprisoned for debt and was very ill. His mother-in-law had described him as 'unstayed' (unstable). There was a history of insanity in his family. His father, William, was seen as a lunatic and a fervent Catholic at a time when that could have cost him his life. At one time William was imprisoned in London for making seditious speeches. It seems quite amazing that the Brookes allowed his son's marriage into their ranks at all.

The pressures from debt, religious belief and those of marriage to a powerful family no doubt weighed heavily. That spring, soon after a local witch trial in the area that saw families set against each other, he snapped. As to why, we'll never know but his mother, Katherine, who had land around

Burton Agnes, was buying more and her wealth grew. She had said that she was not intending to leave any it to her stressed and unbalanced son. The details we have of what happened at the Hall come from a pamphlet published just a few weeks after the murders. Strangely, other legal documentation has not survived and that seems more than coincidence as the Brookes' were in deeper trouble. Lord Brooke was a friend of Sir Walter Raleigh and he followed him into disgrace, being reprieved by James I in December 1603.

The pamphlet paints Calverley as a man under pressure, ranting about his wife's infidelity. Further troubles mount and finally a report that his brother is in gaol that is the last straw. One poor son is promptly stabbed and he loses control totally and raves into his wife's room. In a desperate struggle as she tries to fight him off the children, he wounds her and fatally stabs the other boy. He is finally tracked down, dragged before the magistrate and taken to Wakefield (not York as there was a plague outbreak at the time). Later he was moved to York and kept there until the next assize, but we know just two bare facts about the outcome. First, that he was pressed to death on 5th August, and buried on the same day; and that he was buried in the grounds of St. Mary's. Pressing as a method of execution was slow and barbarous in the extreme. The prisoner would be naked under a board and heavier stones gradually put above to crush them.

Two entries in burial registers tell the story of this Yorkshire tragedy: the first says simply, 'Calverley, St. Wilfrid's 24 April 1605. Wllm. And Walter, sons of Walter Calverley Esq.' The second is more explicit and powerful. 'York, St.Mary's Castlegate 5 Aug. 1605 Walter Calverley executed for murthering unnaturally two of his own children the 23 April 1605.' A.C. Cawley, the literary scholar, points out the lingering fascination about the case. As he notes, Calverley's reasons for remaining mute at the trial are not at all clear. Refusing to plead actually protected his land and stock because the assets were left in a trust, so they would not be lost when the owner committed a felony. Cawley suggests: 'He may have been seeking the speediest way to end his life.' However strange and irrational the criminal act and its surrounding circumstances, if it has potential as an enthralling story, then it is worth finding the emotional heart of the events.

Initially as a researcher of crime, fact or fiction, I was after knowledge rather than a seeker of truth. Now, reflecting back, truth is the real objective.

When I first started writing, I was struck by Mickey Spillane's words: 'There are authors and there are writers.' Learning about crime writing helped me to see that a strong story is foremost; the writer invites the reader to share in the emotion and through its construction.

Told to leave school aged 15 in 1964, because I was never going to be a draughtsman or a fitter in one of the great engineering firms in Leeds, I was not entirely without ability. I had a love of words and gradually started to understand what writing meant to me. Before writing about crime, I felt the impact of Seamus Heaney, a poet I met twice and corresponded with for a time. His poetry taught me that it was acceptable to use the language and the subjects on your doorstep as it were.

Brought up among village folk in Churwell before moving across Leeds to Halton and then Oakwood, I learned from a wider culture before going to Park Lane College part-time and aiming at qualifications. Today, I simply relish telling good stories, the best and most satisfying being those that mix crime and humour, rather than crime and terror.

Murder in Mind

There is an interesting perspective on all crime writing – fact or fiction and that's the contrast between working on the cases before 1920 and on those in more recent times. Until the Modernist writers and artists of the early twentieth century came along, the narratives were all exterior and somehow distanced. They were all of sequential actions and one-dimensional motives. Today, writing and researching, say, the Krays, there is a wealth of secondary material available to the novelist or biographer. Not only is there a retrospective interest in the forensic psychology of their motivations and of their fundamental personalities, but also a growing vocabulary of explanation.

As for Yorkshire, there is much to be said for the richness and diversity of the county when it comes to transgression. In the 1830s, when there was widespread agricultural unrest, there was a long list of arson cases across the East Riding. After the Luddites and with greater industrialisation, with new towns came new crimes and white collar offences proliferated. For the writer and historian, all kinds of frauds and deceptions, along with defamation and new varieties of scams, the twentieth century brought a complexity of subtlety and invention in the devious minds of offenders and criminal masterminds. But on the whole, narratives of drama and mystery persist and appeal, and they always will.

The issue for the writer / researcher is how to get inside and understand, if that is at all possible, the deviant criminal mind; its emotions and motivations at a time of intense pressure and alienation, when it is something never likely to be directly experienced to such a level of destructive behaviour. Abnormal psychology is a factor here and today's crime writer is just as likely to study the textbooks in this area as casebooks and biographies of notorious killers in order to make their work more understandable and compelling. The legal notion of diminished responsibility did not arise until the 1950s and some of the murder cases from that time show the fascination of the 'amoral' as seen in extreme behaviour. The new law had just been passed when 21-year-old Susan Campbell faced a murder charge. Campbell, a Keighley millworker, was babysitting 17-month-old Susan Pickles of Worth Village when the older girl strangled her charge with a belt. Was Campbell a murderer or was it manslaughter? Three days before her trial the legislation came into force.

Under section two of the Homicide Act, 1957, if an accused person is considered to be mentally abnormal to such an extent that this substantially impairs the sense of responsibility, then a reduced charge of applies. Mr Drabble for the prosecution pointed out the guidelines, stressing the point being about 'mental abnormality' but not 'insanity.' The evidence pointed to diminished responsibility applying. Defence lawyer, Geoffrey Veale, told the jury: 'It may be that you are the first jury ever to consider this kind of question that there was some abnormality of mind.' The sentence was life imprisonment but as Campbell was tried in a criminal court, she could have hanged.

It is a disturbing thought that not so long before that date, a condition of epilepsy was not always understood and the legal process adjusted accordingly. Young adults were, on several occasions, sentenced to death before any sound ruling on state of mind and were often reprieved at the last minute. Only four years before the law stating that the minimum age for an offender to be hanged was 16, teenager James Clarkson had the noose wrapped around his neck at Armley for the murder of a twelve-year-old girl. He was heard in prison shouting: 'What made me do it?'

There is still much substance in the standard template

of the true crime story: a tale of excitement, pity and fear from a dastardly deed to retribution. My investigations go on and nothing will ever be as inviting as to set to work on an unsolved case from Yorkshire. For me, the only stipulation for a potential book is that my enquiry should be firmly embedded in distant events. Contemporary stories do not have the same indefinable aura as the murky past, shrouded in darkness and fog; both literal and metaphorical, and the victim disturbingly vulnerable.

SELECT
BIBLIOGRAPHY

Barnard, Sylvia M., *Viewing the Breathless Corpse: coroners and inquests in Victorian Leeds* (Words@Woodmere, 2001)
Bentley, David, *The Sheffield Hanged 1750-1864* (Print and Design, 2002)
Bentley, David, *The Sheffield Murders 1865-1965* (Print and Design, 2003)
Binding, Tim, *On Ilkley Moor* (Picador, 2001)
Bland, James, *The Common Hangman* (Zeon Books, 2001)
Bland, James, *True Crime Diary Vol. 2* (Warner Books, 1999)
Burnley, *James West Riding Sketches* (Hodder and Stoughton, 1875)
Campbell, Marie, *Curious Tales of Old West Yorkshire* (Sigma, 1999)
Campbell, Marie, *Strange World of the Brontes* (Sigma, 2001)
Cawley, A C (Ed.), *A Yorkshire Tragedy* (Manchester University Press, 1986)
Clarke, A A, *Killers at Large* (Arton Books, 1996)
Cornwell, Patricia, *Portrait of a Serial Killer* (Time Warner, 2002)

Murder in Mind

Davies, Owen, *Murder, Magic, Madness: The Victorian trials of Dove and the Wizard* (Pearson, 2005)

Dernley, Syd with Newman, David, *The Hangman's Tale* (Pan, 1989)

Eddleston, John J., *The Encyclopaedia of Executions* (Blake, 2002)

Edwards, Russell, *Naming Jack the Ripper* (Pan Books, 2014)

Ellis, John, *Diary of a Hangman* (Crime Library, 1997)

Emsley, Clive, *Crime and Society in England 1750-1900* (Longman, 1996)

Emsley, Clive, *The English Police – A political and social history* (Pearson 1991)

Evans, Stewart P., *Executioner: The Chronicles of James Berry, Victorian Hangman* (Sutton, 2004)

Fielding, Steve, *Pierrepoint: A Family of Executioners* (John Blake, 2006)

Goodman, David, *Foul Deeds and Suspicious Deaths in Leeds* (Wharncliffe, 2003)

Gould, Russell, *Unsolved Murders* (Virgin, 2002)

Grey, D (Ed. S J Pimm), *The Facts Behind the Guardhouse Murder 1864* (Whins Wood Publishing house, Keighley, 1996)

Harrison, Paul, *Yorkshire Murders* (Countryside, 1992)

Hovell, M, *The Chartist Movement* (Manchester University Press, 1918)

Hughes, Robert, *The Fatal Shore* (Vintage, 2003)

Humphreys, Travers, *Criminal Days* (Hodder and Stoughton, 1946)

Hunt, Tristram, *Building Jerusalem, The rise and fall of the Victorian City* (Phoenix, 2004)

Inglis, Brian, *Poverty and the Industrial Revolution* (Panther, 1971)

James, Mike, *The Bedside Book of Murder* (True Crime Library, 1998)

Jones, Richard Glyn, *True Crime Through History* (Constable, 2004)

Low, Donald A, *The Regency Underworld* (Sutton, 2005)

Macilwee, Michael, *The Teddy Boy Wars* (Milo Books, 2015)

O'Neal, Bill, *The Pimlico Encyclopaedia of Western Gunfighters* (Pimlico, 1998)

Pontefract, Ella and Hartley, Marie, *Yorkshire Tour* (Smith Settle, 2003)

Porter, Roy, *English Society in the Eighteenth Century* (Penguin, 1982)

Porter, Roy, *Madness: A Brief History* (Oxford, 2002)

Rawlings, Philip, *Crime and Power: A History of Criminal Justice* (Longman, 1999)

Roughead, William, *Classic Crimes* (New York Review of Books, 2000)

Rowland, John, *Unfit to Plead?* (Pan, 1965)

Saunders, John B., *Mozley and Whiteley's Law Dictionary* (Butterworths, 1977)

Stevenson, David, *1914-1918 The History of the First World War* (Penguin, 2004)

Thomas, Donald, *The Victorian Underworld* (John Murray, 1998)

Thompson, E P, *The Making of the English Working Class* (Penguin, 1968)

Thornton, David, *Leeds: a historical dictionary of people, places and events* (Northern Heritage Publications, 2013)

Thornton, David, *Leeds: The story of a city* (Fort Publishing, 2002)

Tobias, J J, *Crime and Industrial Society in the Nineteenth Century* (Penguin, 1972)

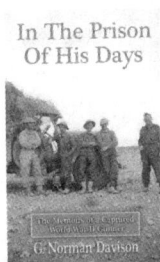

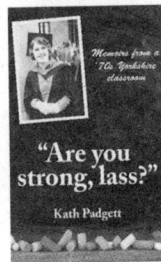

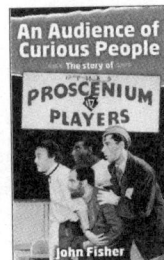

Part political intrigue, part comedic travelogue, an incident-packed memoir that bridges the gap between John le Carré and Johnny English....

"Achieves the rare combination of being instructive and funny..." - Rt. Hon. Alan Johnson MP

Paul Knott

The
Accidental
Diplomat
Adventures in the Foreign Office

Paul Knott is a Northern lad whose working life began on Hull docks, before an improbable career switch to Her Majesty's Diplomatic Service. Here, while globetrotting on official duties, he gets us behind the door of the UK's great offices of state, the Foreign and Commonwealth Office.

Knott's first post is to post-revolutionary Romania, and the eccentricity of a country striving to emerge from the Ceaușescu dictatorship is uproarious.

A superficially more attractive but soulless sojourn in Dubai is enlivened by being abducted at gunpoint by terrorists. His time in the police-state of Uzbekistan is happier, where he takes a hands-on approach to human rights.

A year in Kiev offers a close-up view of the ongoing crisis in Ukraine, plus a few James Bond moments. Finally, he winds up Russia, at a time when an ex-spy is murdered in London by radiation poisoning.

"An engrossing read"
James Brown, Sabotage Times

Investigate our other titles and
stay up to date with all our latest releases at
www.scratchingshedpublishing.co.uk